Healing Your Inner Child

Stop People-Pleasing, Set Healthy Boundaries, and Build Self-Trust

Nancy Willis

Table of Content

Introduction

Every adult carries within them a younger self. This part of us is not gone simply because we've grown older, paid bills, or taken on responsibilities. It lives quietly under the surface, carrying both the joys and the wounds of our earliest years. When that inner child feels ignored, criticized, or unsafe, we see the effects in adulthood— struggling to say no, needing approval, distrusting ourselves, or losing touch with what we truly want.

This book is about repairing that relationship with yourself. It's not about blaming your parents, rewriting history, or pretending childhood didn't shape you. It's about recognizing how early experiences echo in your present life, and learning how to respond with care instead of repeating old patterns.

Many people discover this need when they realize how much time and energy goes into pleasing others. You may notice you agree to things you don't want to do, silence your needs to avoid conflict, or sacrifice your own comfort so someone else feels better. It feels safer in the moment, but it leaves you drained and resentful. The child in you still believes love must be earned through compliance.

Another common sign is difficulty setting boundaries. Saying "no" feels dangerous, as if it will cost you connection or affection. So you keep saying "yes," but the cost is your sense of freedom and respect. Building healthy boundaries is not about pushing people away—it's about allowing yourself to stay connected without losing yourself in the process.

Self-trust is the third pillar of healing. When the inner child has learned that their feelings or instincts are not valid, it becomes hard to make decisions confidently as an adult. You may second-guess yourself, rely heavily on others for advice, or feel paralyzed by choices.

Rebuilding self-trust means learning to listen to your own signals again and proving to yourself that you can handle both success and mistakes.

This book is structured to guide you step by step:

- **Understanding your inner child**—what it is, how it was shaped, and how it shows up now.

- **Recognizing people-pleasing patterns**—where they come from and why they're so hard to let go.

- **Learning boundaries**—what they look like, how to set them, and how to handle the pushback.

- **Rebuilding self-trust**—small daily choices that help you feel safe with yourself again.

- **Integrating these practices** so you can live more authentically and create relationships based on respect and care.

Throughout the chapters, you'll find practical tools: reflection prompts, simple exercises, and examples from real life. Healing is not a quick fix, and no book can erase the past. But you can give yourself what was missing: acceptance, safety, and respect. When the inner child feels seen and supported, you stop living for approval and start living as the adult you were meant to be.

This is the work ahead. It asks for honesty, patience, and courage. But it also offers something deeply rewarding: the freedom to be yourself without apology.

Chapter 1:
Meeting Your Inner Child

Every adult carries a younger self inside them. This is not a metaphor to make childhood seem more sentimental than it was; it is a psychological truth. The "inner child" refers to the emotional imprint left by our earliest years—the feelings, beliefs, and memories that shaped our sense of self before we had the words or reasoning to explain them. Even if decades have passed, those early impressions remain active, influencing how we think, behave, and relate to others.

Meeting your inner child means becoming aware of this part of yourself and learning how it shows up in your life today. For some people, the inner child feels hidden away, buried under years of responsibilities and busyness. For others, it appears more obviously through anxiety, anger, or a constant drive to please others. Understanding this inner presence is the first step toward healing.

Why the Inner Child Matters

Childhood experiences are not just memories; they are blueprints. The way we were treated taught us how to view ourselves and what to expect from others. If love felt conditional—based on obedience, performance, or silence—we may grow into adults who believe our worth depends on what we do rather than who we are. If our emotions were ignored or ridiculed, we may learn to hide them, only to discover later that hiding makes intimacy nearly impossible.

These lessons operate beneath the surface. You may not consciously think, *I'm unworthy unless I make others happy*, but your choices reveal it: saying yes when you want to say no, apologizing for things that aren't your fault, or overworking yourself to avoid criticism.

When this happens, it isn't the rational adult making the decision—it's the inner child still trying to secure safety and love.

Signs Your Inner Child Is Calling Out

People often ask, "How do I know if I need to work on my inner child?" The truth is that everyone has an inner child, but not everyone realizes when it is wounded. Some of the most common signs include:

- **Excessive people-pleasing.** Constantly putting others' needs ahead of your own, often to the point of exhaustion.

- **Fear of rejection or abandonment.** Anxiety that others will leave or dislike you if you set limits or show your true feelings.

- **Difficulty trusting yourself.** Second-guessing decisions, relying heavily on others' opinions, or avoiding choices altogether.

- **Emotional flashbacks.** Feeling disproportionately upset, ashamed, or panicked in situations that echo old childhood wounds.

- **Low self-worth.** Believing you're never enough, no matter how much you accomplish.

None of these patterns appear out of thin air. They are traces of a child who adapted to survive in an environment that did not fully meet their emotional needs. Healing means recognizing that these old strategies no longer serve you.

Meeting the Inner Child with Curiosity

The goal is not to blame your parents or rewrite the past but to acknowledge the child you once were and the child who still lives inside you. Think of this less as an intellectual project and more as a relationship. Just as you would approach a real child with patience and curiosity, you can approach your inner child in the same way.

9

A simple exercise is to picture yourself at a young age—five, six, or seven years old. What did you look like? What kinds of things made you laugh or cry? What was missing that you longed for? Many people find it moving, even unsettling, to realize that younger version of themselves still lingers inside. But it is through this awareness that healing becomes possible.

How the Inner Child Affects Adult Relationships

Unacknowledged wounds do not disappear; they get replayed. For instance, if you grew up feeling responsible for keeping peace in the family, you may carry that habit into friendships and romantic relationships. You might avoid conflict at all costs, suppress your feelings, or work tirelessly to ensure everyone else is comfortable, even if it leaves you depleted.

Similarly, if your emotions were dismissed when you were young, you may find it hard to express vulnerability now. Instead, you might keep others at a distance or cling too tightly, fearing abandonment. These are not signs of weakness; they are signs of an inner child still waiting for the safety and acceptance they never received.

When you begin to see these patterns not as flaws but as survival strategies, compassion naturally grows. Instead of criticizing yourself for being "too sensitive" or "too needy," you start to understand why those tendencies exist. That understanding is what allows change.

Opening the Door to Healing

Meeting your inner child is only the beginning. Healing involves listening, responding, and offering what was missing—whether that is comfort, protection, or permission to be fully yourself. Some people use journaling, others use guided meditations, and many work with therapists to support this process. The method matters less than the intention: to bring the child inside you out of the shadows and into a relationship with the adult you are now.

When you acknowledge your inner child, you reclaim the parts of yourself that were silenced. You begin to notice when you are acting from old fear rather than present reality. And with practice, you can choose differently. You can say no without panic, express needs without shame, and trust your own decisions.

A New Beginning

This chapter sets the foundation for everything that follows. To heal, you must first recognize what you are healing. The inner child is not a weakness, nor is it a burden. It is a part of you that wants to be seen and valued. By meeting this child with compassion and curiosity, you begin to shift from living on autopilot—reacting to old wounds—to living consciously as the adult you are today.

The chapters ahead will guide you through specific patterns—people-pleasing, weak boundaries, lack of self-trust—and show you how to break them. But none of that work is possible without first meeting the child within. This is the part of you that longs for care, safety, and freedom. When you give it to yourself, you unlock the possibility of living without apology.

What the Inner Child Really Is

When people first hear the phrase "inner child," it often sounds abstract, maybe even sentimental. Some imagine it as nothing more than a metaphor, while others picture it as a poetic way of talking about childhood memories. But the inner child is not simply an idea you read about in self-help books. It is a real psychological presence that continues to live within each of us, shaping how we feel, react, and connect with others.

The inner child can be understood as the emotional self that developed during your earliest years. It carries not only your joyful memories—the laughter, the playfulness, the curiosity—but also the pain and confusion that arose when your needs were not met. Because children lack the language and perspective to process experiences, those early emotions often remain raw and unfiltered. They get stored deep inside, forming the foundation for how you see yourself and how you believe the world works.

This part of you doesn't vanish simply because you grow older, graduate, or step into adult responsibilities. The child within remains active, and in moments of stress or intimacy, it often surfaces without warning. You might find yourself suddenly anxious when someone raises their voice, even if the situation is harmless. You may notice yourself shrinking back in conversations, trying hard not to upset anyone. You may crave approval so strongly that you sacrifice your own needs to get it. These reactions are not irrational—they are the voice of the child inside you, still doing its best to feel safe.

Understanding the inner child also helps explain why logical reasoning doesn't always solve our problems. You might know, on a rational level, that setting a boundary is healthy. Yet when you try to say no, your body floods with guilt and fear. That's because the part of you responding is not the adult who has learned about boundaries but the child who once believed that saying no would risk love or connection. Healing the inner child means addressing that younger part directly instead of trying to out-argue it with adult logic.

One way to think about this is to picture your inner world as a house. Your adult self lives in the present, in the rooms you've decorated and chosen. But in the basement of that house lives the younger version of you, still holding the emotions you couldn't handle years ago. You may avoid going down there because it feels overwhelming, or you may not even realize the basement exists. Yet the child is there, influencing the atmosphere of the entire house. Meeting your inner child is like turning on the light, opening the door, and beginning to listen.

The inner child shows up in more ways than we usually realize. Sometimes it appears in moments of joy—when you feel spontaneous, playful, or deeply moved by something simple. Other times it appears in pain—when criticism cuts more deeply than it should, when rejection feels unbearable, or when you act out of fear instead of choice. These are signals that the younger part of you is present and asking for attention.

It's important to understand that the inner child is not your enemy. Many people become frustrated when they notice themselves repeating old patterns: giving in, staying silent, or doubting themselves. They say, "Why do I keep doing this? I should know better." But those patterns are the strategies your younger self created to survive. A child may have learned that being quiet kept them safe from anger, or that being helpful earned them affection. While those strategies once served a purpose, they are now outdated. The task is not to condemn them but to thank the child for trying to protect you, and then gently show that child a different way.

Working with the inner child requires a shift in how you see yourself. Instead of treating your struggles as character flaws, you begin to see them as unfinished business from your early years. You start to view yourself with compassion, as you would a real child who did their best with limited tools. This shift is powerful because it changes the conversation from "What's wrong with me?" to "What does my younger self still need?"

Sometimes people resist the idea of the inner child because it feels uncomfortable to revisit the past. They fear that acknowledging this younger part will trap them in old wounds. But the opposite is true. Ignoring the inner child keeps you stuck in patterns you don't understand. Facing the child within allows you to heal and move forward with more freedom. It is not about living in the past but about freeing the present from the grip of unresolved pain.

The first step is simply recognition. Take a moment to recall yourself at a young age—perhaps five, six, or seven. What did you look like? What made you happy? What frightened you? How did you try to get love or avoid trouble? These reflections are not just memories; they are doorways into the part of you that still longs to be seen. By remembering that child, you begin to bridge the distance between who you were and who you are.

As you continue through this book, the inner child will become less of an abstract idea and more of a companion you can understand, comfort, and support. Meeting this part of yourself is not an act of indulgence—it is an act of responsibility. You cannot undo the past, but you can offer yourself now what you needed then: safety, understanding, and care. Recognizing the child inside you is the beginning of real change, because only when you see the source of your pain can you choose a new way forward.

How Childhood Shapes the Adult Self

The years of childhood may feel far away, but their influence lingers in every corner of adult life. We often like to think that growing up means leaving the past behind, yet the truth is that much of what we believe, fear, and strive for today was learned long before we were aware of learning anything at all. Childhood does not just provide a set of memories; it builds the lens through which we see the world and ourselves.

The early environment teaches us what love looks like. If affection was given freely, we may grow up with the sense that we are worthy simply for existing. If affection had to be earned through performance, obedience, or pleasing behavior, we may learn that worth is conditional. That belief, once formed, becomes the background assumption in adult relationships. A partner's silence might trigger panic. A friend's criticism might feel unbearable. These intense reactions are not just about the present moment—they are echoes of lessons absorbed years ago.

How adults treated us also shaped our relationship with emotions. Some children grow up in households where feelings were dismissed or ridiculed. A child who cried may have been told to "toughen up" or "stop being dramatic." Over time, that child learns that expressing pain is unsafe. As an adult, they may struggle to communicate needs, often hiding feelings until they boil over. Others may have grown up in environments where emotions were overwhelming—perhaps a parent's anger or despair dominated the home. Those children might learn to fear emotions altogether, avoiding conflict or shutting down whenever intensity arises.

These early experiences also influence how we see authority and safety. If caregivers were unpredictable or harsh, the child's nervous system adapts by becoming hyper-alert. This heightened vigilance may later appear as anxiety, perfectionism, or people-pleasing. On the other hand, if caregivers were nurturing but also overly controlling, a child might grow up doubting their own judgment, always waiting for someone else to decide what is right. In both cases, the adult self is shaped less by conscious choice and more by the survival strategies learned in those formative years.

What makes childhood so powerful is the way the brain develops. Young children are like sponges, absorbing not only information but also emotional patterns. They don't yet have the reasoning skills to challenge what they see or hear. If a parent constantly criticizes, the child does not think, *My parent is wrong.* Instead, the child concludes, *Something must be wrong with me.* That conclusion sinks in at a level deeper than thought. It becomes part of identity.

This explains why certain challenges persist even when we "know better." You might understand, on an intellectual level, that you deserve respect, yet find yourself tolerating disrespect in relationships. You might recognize that rest is healthy, yet feel guilty when you're not productive. The struggle is not with logic—it is with beliefs planted long before you had the tools to question them. The inner child still carries those beliefs, and unless addressed, they continue to run the show from behind the scenes.

The good news is that childhood does not just leave scars; it also leaves strengths. Many adults underestimate the resilience they developed as children. A person who grew up in chaos may have cultivated deep empathy and sensitivity to others' needs. Someone who had to adapt quickly may now have strong problem-solving skills. The task of healing is not to erase the past but to recognize which lessons still serve you and which ones keep you stuck.

Consider how this plays out in relationships. If you learned early that love is earned through sacrifice, you might overextend yourself with friends, partners, or colleagues. You give and give, hoping to secure acceptance, but feel drained and resentful. This is not a random flaw—it is the child within still trying to repeat the old formula for safety. On the other hand, if you grew up encouraged to express yourself, you may bring openness and honesty into your adult connections, creating healthier bonds. Both patterns, positive and negative, come from the same source: the shaping force of childhood.

Workplaces reflect this shaping too. The employee who cannot stop saying yes to extra tasks may be replaying the childhood role of the "good kid" who earned approval through compliance. The manager who reacts defensively to feedback may still be carrying the sting of constant criticism from a parent. Meanwhile, the person who learned early to trust their instincts may thrive in leadership, confident in their decisions. Again, these are not random traits; they are extensions of childhood lessons.

Even our relationship with ourselves is influenced by those early years. Some adults push themselves relentlessly because they learned as children that rest equaled laziness. Others sabotage opportunities because deep down they believe success will only draw more criticism. These patterns can feel frustrating, as though some invisible hand is holding you back. In reality, it is not an external force—it is the child inside you, still living by outdated rules.

The role of healing, then, is to update the script. Just as a child needs guidance to learn that the world is safe, your inner child needs reassurance that the old lessons are no longer true. The adult you are today has access to resources, choices, and perspectives that were unavailable back then. By revisiting those early patterns with compassion rather than judgment, you can begin to release what no longer serves you.

It helps to think of childhood as the soil in which you were planted. Some soil was rich and supportive, helping you grow strong. Some soil was rocky or depleted, forcing you to adapt in ways that limited your growth. But as an adult, you are no longer stuck in the same ground. You can choose to replant yourself in healthier soil, to tend to the parts of you that were neglected, and to nurture the growth that was stunted. Recognizing how childhood shaped you is the first step toward making those choices.

Childhood may be behind you, but its imprint remains. By understanding how those early years formed the blueprint of your adult self, you gain the power to decide which parts of that blueprint you want to keep and which you are ready to redesign. This awareness doesn't erase the past, but it gives you something more valuable: the freedom to live your present life as an adult, rather than unconsciously repeating the patterns of a child.

Signs of a Wounded Inner Child

Many adults sense that something inside them feels unsettled, but they can't always put words to it. They notice patterns that repeat— saying yes when they want to say no, feeling small in the face of criticism, or craving approval long after they've achieved success. These are not random habits or quirks. They are signals from the inner child, pointing to old wounds that were never healed. Recognizing these signs is not about labeling yourself as broken. It is about understanding the places where your younger self still holds pain and learning how that pain continues to shape your present.

One of the most common signs of a wounded inner child is people-pleasing. This shows up as an almost automatic reflex to prioritize others' comfort, even at your own expense. You might hear yourself agreeing to commitments you don't have time for or smiling politely while someone crosses your boundaries. Deep down, there's often a fear that saying no or asserting yourself will lead to rejection. This isn't because you are weak or indecisive. It is because the child you once were believed that love or safety depended on compliance. That belief still whispers in your ear, urging you to stay agreeable no matter the cost.

Another signal is a strong fear of abandonment. You may feel anxious when someone doesn't reply to your message right away, or panicked if a partner seems distant. The adult part of you might know it's unreasonable, but the inner child feels the possibility of being left as dangerous and unbearable. This can lead to clinging behaviors in relationships or, conversely, pushing people away to avoid the risk of rejection altogether. Both responses trace back to the same root: a child who never felt fully secure in their connection with caregivers.

A wounded inner child also shows itself through difficulty trusting yourself. Many adults carry an ongoing sense of doubt, constantly second-guessing their decisions. You might find yourself paralyzed by choices, replaying every possible outcome in your head, or endlessly seeking reassurance from others. This comes from a history where your feelings or instincts were not validated. If as a child you were told that what you felt was wrong or that your ideas didn't matter, you may have learned to ignore your inner signals. The adult who emerges from that environment struggles to believe their own voice is reliable.

Emotional intensity can also reveal the presence of old wounds. You may find yourself reacting with disproportionate anger, shame, or sadness to situations that seem minor. A comment from a colleague might trigger days of self-criticism. A partner's neutral tone might send you spiraling with worry. These are not simply overreactions; they are emotional flashbacks. The nervous system remembers earlier experiences, and when something in the present resembles those old conditions, the child within responds as if the past is happening again.

Low self-worth is another sign that the inner child is hurting. Adults with unhealed wounds often live with the belief that no matter what they achieve, it isn't enough. Promotions, degrees, or praise may bring temporary relief but never lasting satisfaction. The child inside learned to measure worth against impossible standards—perhaps through constant comparison, criticism, or lack of recognition. That belief persists, driving the adult to chase approval while secretly feeling undeserving of it.

Perfectionism often grows out of these wounds as well. For some, it becomes a way of avoiding shame: if you do everything flawlessly, no one can criticize you. For others, it is a strategy for earning love: if you excel, you will be accepted. On the surface, perfectionism may look like discipline or ambition, but underneath it is the scared voice of a child who believes mistakes are dangerous. The problem is that perfection is unattainable, so the adult is left exhausted, never feeling safe enough to rest.

Sometimes the signs of a wounded inner child show up in more subtle ways. You might struggle with intimacy, finding it difficult to let others truly know you. You might avoid conflict so intensely that you sacrifice honesty in your relationships. Or you might swing between overdependence and withdrawal, never quite sure how close is too close. These patterns can confuse both you and the people around you, but they make sense when you see them as attempts by your inner child to protect you from repeating past hurts.

It is also possible for the wounded child to show up in behaviors that seem opposite of vulnerability. Some people become controlling, defensive, or quick to anger. These adults may appear strong on the outside, but the forcefulness often masks a deep fear of being powerless, just as they once felt in childhood. Behind the shield of aggression is a younger self still terrified of being hurt again.

Recognizing these signs is not about blaming your past or excusing your present actions. It is about connecting the dots so that you can respond differently. When you catch yourself people-pleasing, you can pause and ask, *What is my inner child afraid of right now?* When you notice panic rising at the thought of rejection, you can remind yourself, *This fear belongs to an earlier time. I am safe now.* These small shifts mark the beginning of healing, because they bring the child's voice out of the shadows and into conscious awareness.

The most important thing to remember is that these patterns are not proof of weakness or failure. They are proof of resilience. The wounded child inside you found ways to cope, even in environments that felt unsafe or unkind. Those strategies helped you survive, and that deserves respect. But survival strategies are not the same as thriving. By recognizing the signs of a wounded inner child, you give yourself the chance to move beyond survival into a fuller, freer way of living.

These signals are invitations, not verdicts. They are the child within tugging at your sleeve, asking to be noticed, asking for comfort and care. When you pay attention to them, you no longer have to repeat the same cycles unconsciously. You begin to bring the past into the light, where healing becomes possible.

Beginning the Connection

Acknowledging that an inner child exists is only the starting point. The real work begins when you decide to reach out and build a relationship with that younger part of yourself. This is not about pretending or playing make-believe. It is about learning to listen inwardly, to offer the care and attention that may have been missing in your early years. Establishing this connection can feel unfamiliar at first, but it opens the door to healing patterns that have followed you for decades.

The first step is willingness. You don't need to know exactly how to "do" inner child work, and you don't have to force yourself into deep emotional states. What matters most is a genuine openness to meet the younger version of yourself with kindness. That shift alone changes everything. Instead of ignoring uncomfortable feelings or criticizing yourself for overreacting, you start to ask: *What does the child in me need right now?*

A practical way to begin is through visualization. Choose a quiet moment, close your eyes, and picture yourself at an age when life felt particularly vulnerable—perhaps five, six, or seven years old. Notice the details: your expression, your posture, the clothes you wore. Then gently imagine sitting down with that child. How does the child look at you? What emotions come up as you see them? This exercise is not about forcing a scripted conversation but about allowing your mind to reconnect with a version of you that still lives inside. Even if it feels awkward, the act of turning your attention inward is powerful in itself.

Journaling can also help. Write a letter to your younger self, telling them what you wish they had heard back then. For example: *You were never too much. Your feelings were real. You did not have to earn love—you deserved it all along.* Writing in this way bypasses the rational adult voice and speaks directly to the child within. Over time, journaling creates a dialogue, where you can ask your inner child questions and record the responses that come up, whether as words, images, or emotions.

Some people find that the connection grows strongest in daily life, not just in set exercises. Pay attention to moments when you feel small, scared, or overwhelmed. Instead of pushing those feelings away, pause and imagine what the child in you is experiencing. Maybe they're afraid of being scolded, or maybe they're longing for reassurance. Respond to that child with gentleness. Place a hand over your heart, take a deep breath, and silently say, *I'm here with you. You're safe now.* These simple gestures create a sense of inner safety that may have been missing before.

Another way to begin is through playfulness. The inner child does not only carry wounds; it also holds joy, curiosity, and creativity. Reconnecting with this side of yourself can be just as healing as addressing pain. Think about what you loved as a child—drawing, singing, running outside, building with blocks. Allow yourself to do those things again, not for productivity or achievement, but simply for pleasure. Giving your inner child space to play communicates that life is not only about responsibility. It reminds you both that joy is allowed.

Resistance often shows up when starting this work. You may feel silly talking to your younger self, or you may notice an inner voice saying, *This is pointless.* That resistance is natural. Many adults were taught to dismiss their emotions or "be tough," so approaching themselves with gentleness feels foreign. If this happens, don't force the process. Acknowledge the discomfort, then return to the practice later. Remember: the goal is not to perform perfectly but to slowly build trust with yourself.

Trust is central here. Just as real children need consistency to feel safe, your inner child will respond to repeated care over time. If you only check in occasionally, you may not notice much change. But if you make a habit of asking how your inner child feels, offering comfort, and giving space for expression, you will start to see shifts. Patterns that once felt automatic—people-pleasing, self-doubt, avoidance—become easier to notice and interrupt. This happens because the child inside finally feels seen, no longer forced to shout through anxiety or shame to get your attention.

Support from others can deepen the connection as well. Sharing your process with a trusted friend, partner, or therapist helps normalize the experience. Sometimes saying out loud, *There's a part of me that still feels like a scared kid,* reduces the shame around it. Hearing understanding or encouragement from someone else reinforces the message you are trying to give yourself: it's okay to have needs, it's okay to feel.

Patience is perhaps the most important ingredient. The inner child does not open up on command. Just as a real child would not instantly trust a stranger, the younger you may hesitate at first. Years of neglect, dismissal, or criticism cannot be undone overnight. But with steady, gentle attention, the child begins to believe that the adult self is truly there to listen and protect. Healing unfolds gradually, like a friendship built on repeated moments of care.

Beginning the connection is not about fixing everything at once. It is about creating space for the child in you to exist without judgment. When you visualize, write, play, or pause in moments of stress, you are telling that younger self: *You are not alone anymore. I am here with you.* That message, repeated over time, changes the way you relate to yourself and to others. It reduces the grip of old fears and allows a more authentic, grounded version of you to emerge.

This chapter has introduced you to the inner child, explained how childhood shaped your adult self, outlined the signs of unhealed wounds, and offered starting points for connection. As you move into the next chapter, keep in mind that the patterns you'll be exploring—like people-pleasing—are not flaws but adaptations. They were created by a child who wanted nothing more than to feel safe and loved. By meeting that child now, you give yourself the chance to finally break free from those old strategies and begin living with more honesty and trust.

Chapter 2:
The Roots of People-Pleasing

The habit of putting everyone else first may look like generosity, but beneath it often lies fear. People-pleasing is one of the most common ways a wounded inner child shows up in adult life. It is not simply about being nice or cooperative. It is about trading your needs for approval, believing that harmony is more important than honesty, and that love must be earned by sacrifice. To understand this behavior, we need to look at where it begins.

Most patterns of people-pleasing start in childhood. A child depends completely on caregivers for survival. If those caregivers respond with warmth and acceptance, the child feels safe being authentic. But if care is inconsistent—if affection is given only when the child behaves, achieves, or stays quiet—the child learns that love is conditional. To keep connection, they adjust. They become helpful, agreeable, and undemanding, even at the cost of their own needs. Over time, these adjustments become ingrained, long after the child grows up.

This survival strategy makes sense in the context of childhood. For a child, losing approval can feel as dangerous as losing shelter. If staying invisible kept arguments from escalating, the child learned silence. If praise came only with good grades, the child learned perfectionism. If love appeared when others were comfortable, the child learned to monitor everyone else's moods more carefully than their own. Each adaptation was an attempt to secure safety in an environment that felt unpredictable.

The problem arises when those adaptations carry into adulthood. The adult who once learned to avoid conflict may now struggle to assert themselves at work or in relationships. The adult who was praised for being selfless may ignore their own exhaustion until it turns into resentment. The child who equated love with performance may still push themselves relentlessly, afraid that slowing down will cost them affection. These patterns are not chosen freely. They are the echoes of lessons learned before the adult had a choice.

People-pleasing also becomes reinforced by culture. Many societies praise self-sacrifice, politeness, and productivity. Adults who constantly give more than they have are often admired, not questioned. "She's so reliable," colleagues might say, without noticing that reliability comes at the cost of rest. "He never complains," friends might note, unaware that silence hides unmet needs. What looks like virtue is often a mask hiding fear. The culture rewards the mask, which makes it even harder to take it off.

The cost of people-pleasing, however, is heavy. At first it may bring temporary peace: no one is upset, everyone is satisfied, and you feel safe. But the price is your authenticity. Each time you silence your needs or agree against your will, you send yourself the message that your truth does not matter. Over years, this erodes self-trust. You may lose touch with what you actually want, because you are so practiced at scanning others for clues. You may feel resentment growing in relationships that seem outwardly harmonious. You may notice exhaustion from carrying the emotional weight of everyone else.

Another hidden cost is the constant anxiety of maintaining approval. Because the people-pleaser depends on external validation, their sense of worth rises and falls with others' reactions. A compliment may bring relief, but one critical word can spiral into shame. Approval becomes addictive—never enough, always temporary. No matter how much you give, the security doesn't last.

Breaking free from this pattern begins with recognizing that it developed for good reasons. The child who learned to please was not weak. They were resourceful, adapting in the only way they could to preserve connection. Honoring that resourcefulness is important,

26

because it removes shame from the process. You cannot change what you do not first accept.

The next step is to question whether the strategy still serves you. As an adult, you have more choices than you did as a child. You are no longer dependent on others for survival. Yet the inner child still acts as if saying no will endanger you. By gently bringing awareness to these moments, you can begin to reassure that younger part of yourself: *I am safe now. I can set limits. I can survive disapproval.*

This does not mean becoming harsh or indifferent to others. True connection thrives on honesty, not compliance. When you say yes from a place of choice rather than fear, your relationships gain depth. When you allow others to meet you as you are, not as you perform to be, you discover which connections are real and which depend on your silence. Boundaries do not end relationships—they filter them, allowing only those that can handle the truth of who you are.

People-pleasing has roots in childhood, but its branches spread through adult life, shaping decisions, careers, and relationships. By tracing those roots back, you begin to see that what felt like a flaw is actually an old survival skill. It kept you safe once, but now it keeps you small. Healing means thanking the child who tried so hard to belong, while teaching the adult that belonging no longer requires erasure. Approval may feel comforting, but it is no substitute for authenticity. Real safety comes from being able to stand in your truth, even when others disapprove.

Why People-Pleasing Develops

At first glance, people-pleasing can look like nothing more than politeness or kindness. You say yes when asked for help, you try to avoid conflict, you go out of your way to make sure others feel comfortable. But when these behaviors are driven by fear rather than choice, they stop being generosity and become self-erasure. To understand why people-pleasing develops, we have to look back at the conditions in which it first takes root: childhood.

Every child needs safety, love, and belonging. When these needs are consistently met, the child grows with the sense that being themselves is enough. But when care feels conditional—when approval depends on behavior, performance, or silence—the child adapts. That adaptation often looks like compliance. If being agreeable prevents conflict, the child learns to agree. If being helpful earns praise, the child learns to help. If staying quiet avoids punishment, the child learns to silence their own voice. These adjustments are not signs of weakness but strategies for survival.

Think of a child in a household where anger erupts unpredictably. Maybe a parent lashes out when things don't go their way. In that environment, the safest path is to avoid becoming a target. The child becomes skilled at reading moods, softening their own presence, and smoothing over tension before it escalates. Years later, that child has grown into an adult who still monitors every room they enter, making sure not to upset anyone. The context has changed, but the habit remains.

Or imagine a child whose worth was tied to achievement. They were praised when they got top grades, scored goals, or performed well in recitals, but ignored or criticized when they fell short. The lesson absorbed is simple: love comes through excellence. That child becomes an adult who works tirelessly, afraid to slow down, convinced that rest equals failure. The pattern looks like ambition, but underneath it is fear of rejection.

People-pleasing can also arise from subtle forms of neglect. When children grow up feeling invisible—when their feelings aren't noticed or their voices aren't heard—they may conclude that the best way to keep connection is to adapt to what others want. They stop asking, *What do I need?* and instead ask, *What will keep me close to others?*

This shift might preserve attachment, but it costs authenticity. By adulthood, these individuals may not even know what their own preferences are, because they've spent years shaping themselves around the expectations of others.

Culture can deepen these tendencies. Many children are told directly or indirectly that being "good" means being compliant. Boys may be praised for toughness and self-reliance, while girls are often rewarded for being sweet, agreeable, and accommodating. These gendered expectations reinforce the belief that pleasing others is a virtue. Some children internalize these lessons so deeply that they never stop to question whether the constant giving is actually healthy.

Family roles also play a part. In households marked by dysfunction—addiction, conflict, or instability—children sometimes take on the role of the caretaker or peacemaker. They learn to manage the emotional climate, to step in and soothe others, to anticipate needs before they are spoken. While these skills can look admirable, they often leave the child emotionally neglected. The adult who emerges from this role may feel compelled to fix or rescue everyone around them, even when it drains their own energy.

Another factor is the human nervous system itself. As children, we are wired to attach to caregivers because survival depends on it. When those caregivers are inconsistent or frightening, the nervous system adapts by finding ways to maintain closeness. People-pleasing is one such adaptation. The child's body associates compliance with safety. That association becomes automatic, carried into adulthood where the stakes are no longer survival but still feel just as urgent.

The development of people-pleasing is also linked to shame. When children are shamed for expressing needs—told they are selfish, dramatic, or too sensitive—they internalize the belief that their natural impulses are wrong. To avoid the sting of shame, they suppress those impulses. Pleasing others becomes a shield against feeling unworthy. The problem is that while it may protect from immediate disapproval, it also erases the authentic self.

It's important to stress that these patterns do not mean something is "wrong" with you. They mean that as a child, you adapted brilliantly to your environment. You found a way to secure connection and reduce harm. In that sense, people-pleasing is a success story of survival. But what kept you safe as a child may now keep you stuck as an adult. The same strategies that once preserved belonging can now prevent intimacy, fulfillment, and self-respect.

When you catch yourself slipping into automatic yeses, avoiding conflict, or worrying excessively about what others think, it helps to pause and ask: *Where did I learn this?* Often, the answer traces back to those early moments where you believed safety depended on being agreeable. Naming this origin doesn't immediately erase the habit, but it reframes it. Instead of seeing yourself as weak or indecisive, you see a child who tried to survive. From that compassion, change becomes possible.

The roots of people-pleasing are deep, planted in childhood soil that may have been rocky, unpredictable, or demanding. But being aware of those roots is the first step in loosening their grip. You can begin to tell yourself a new story: that safety and love no longer depend on erasing your needs. As an adult, you have choices the child never had. You can begin to set limits, to voice your truth, and to trust that real connection doesn't require constant self-sacrifice.

The Hidden Costs of Always Saying Yes

On the surface, saying yes seems harmless—even admirable. You agree to help a friend move, you stay late at work to finish a project, you accept an invitation even when you're exhausted. These choices may look like kindness or dedication, and sometimes they are. But when yes becomes automatic, when it overrides your true feelings and needs, it carries a heavy price. The hidden costs of people-pleasing accumulate slowly, often unnoticed until they leave you drained, resentful, and disconnected from yourself.

One of the most immediate costs is exhaustion. Constantly meeting the needs of others requires energy that you may not have to spare. The body feels the strain through fatigue, headaches, or tension that never fully releases. You might collapse at the end of the day, wondering why you feel so tired when nothing seemed particularly difficult. The answer is that your energy wasn't spent on what nourishes you; it was spent on managing the comfort of everyone else.

Another cost is resentment. At first, saying yes may feel satisfying. You've avoided conflict, earned appreciation, or secured temporary peace. But over time, an unspoken anger begins to build. You start to notice how often others rely on you, how little space is left for your needs, and how invisible your own limits feel. This resentment can poison relationships. Outwardly, you may still smile and comply, but inside, frustration grows. The longer it goes unaddressed, the more it risks exploding in ways that surprise both you and those around you.

Loss of identity is another subtle but profound consequence. When you spend years bending to others, you can lose touch with what you truly want. Simple questions—What do I feel like eating? How do I want to spend my weekend?—can become strangely difficult to answer. The voice of the inner child, trained to scan for others' expectations, drowns out your own preferences. As a result, you may feel hollow, like you're living someone else's life rather than your own.

Always saying yes also erodes self-trust. Each time you override your inner signals, you send yourself the message that your needs don't matter. Eventually, you may stop listening altogether. This creates a painful cycle: you don't trust your feelings, so you look outward for cues, which deepens your dependence on others' approval. The more you rely on external validation, the more fragile your sense of worth becomes. A compliment might lift you, but criticism can devastate you, because your identity rests on shaky ground.

The costs extend to physical health as well. Chronic people-pleasing often leads to stress-related conditions: anxiety, insomnia, digestive issues, even weakened immunity. The body keeps score of the times you pushed past exhaustion, ignored hunger, or silenced emotional pain. Over years, this constant self-suppression takes a toll, leaving the body depleted and vulnerable. What looks like harmless politeness is, in truth, a long-term strain on your system.

Relationships suffer too. Ironically, people-pleasing often undermines the very connections it's meant to protect. When you say yes out of fear rather than honesty, intimacy weakens. Others never get to know the real you—they only know the agreeable version you present. This can attract people who exploit your compliance, while pushing away those who want authentic connection. Healthy relationships require boundaries, and without them, closeness becomes lopsided, built on performance instead of truth.

Another hidden cost is missed opportunities. Each unnecessary yes closes the door to something else—time for rest, space for creativity, or chances to pursue your own goals. When your schedule is packed with commitments that don't reflect your desires, your life drifts off course. You may wake up one day realizing that years have passed in service of others' expectations, while your own dreams have been postponed indefinitely.

Perhaps the deepest cost of all is the quiet message you internalize: that you are only valuable when useful. This belief eats away at self-worth, making it harder to accept love freely. You may find yourself suspicious of affection, wondering if people like you for who you are or for what you provide. The tragedy of constant yes is that it convinces you that being yourself is not enough.

Breaking this cycle begins with awareness. Start noticing when you say yes automatically. Ask yourself: *Do I truly want to do this, or am I afraid of what will happen if I say no?* The answer can be revealing. Often, the fear is not about the task itself but about the imagined consequences—disapproval, rejection, or conflict. Recognizing this distinction is the first step toward reclaiming choice.

It also helps to reframe what saying no means. Many people equate no with selfishness, but in reality, no is often the most honest answer. It creates space for your yes to carry weight. When you agree because you genuinely want to, not because you feel pressured, others can trust that your presence is real. Boundaries don't diminish generosity—they protect it, ensuring that your giving comes from fullness rather than depletion.

The costs of people-pleasing are real, but they are not irreversible. Each time you pause before agreeing, each time you honor your limits, you begin to rebuild self-trust. Relationships may shift as you practice this, but those shifts reveal which connections can handle your authenticity. The people who truly care will respect your boundaries. Those who can't may drift away, and while that loss can feel painful, it also clears space for healthier bonds.

Saying yes has its place. Acts of service, kindness, and cooperation are beautiful parts of human connection. But when yes is driven by fear, it becomes a cage. By recognizing the hidden costs, you can begin to step out of that cage and discover what life feels like when your choices reflect not only others' comfort but also your own truth.

How People-Pleasing Shows Up in Daily Life

People-pleasing is often easier to recognize in others than in ourselves. We tell a friend, *You don't always have to say yes,* but fail to notice how often we do the same. Because the habit becomes automatic, it blends into daily routines until we think it's just part of who we are. Looking closely, though, the signs appear everywhere—in conversations, decisions, and even in the silence we keep.

At work, people-pleasing might look like volunteering for extra tasks even when your plate is already full. You stay late, answer emails at night, or take responsibility for things that aren't yours. On the outside, it looks like dedication. Inside, it often comes from fear: fear of disappointing a boss, fear of being seen as lazy, or fear of losing your job if you don't overdeliver. Over time, this pattern leaves you exhausted and makes it harder for others to respect your boundaries, because you've trained them to expect endless availability.

In friendships, the behavior can show up as always being the one who listens but never sharing your own struggles. You nod, comfort, and offer support, but when it comes to your needs, you stay quiet. You don't want to "burden" anyone or risk being seen as difficult. The result is an uneven relationship where you play the role of caretaker rather than equal partner.

Romantic relationships bring their own version of this pattern. Many people-pleasers struggle to express preferences—where to eat, how to spend weekends, even what kind of intimacy they want. Instead of voicing their truth, they defer to their partner. At first, this may seem like flexibility, but over time, it creates distance. A partner can sense when you're not fully present, when your yes isn't genuine. This silence can lead to frustration on both sides: you feel unseen, and they feel the absence of your real self.

Family dynamics often reveal the deepest roots. Around parents or siblings, old roles resurface easily. You might revert to being the "good child," the mediator, or the one who never makes trouble. Even if you've built independence in other areas, a holiday dinner can bring back the urge to smooth over conflict, laugh at jokes that hurt, or hide opinions that go against the family script. The inner child is quick to reappear when surrounded by the people who shaped the original pattern.

Social situations show smaller but equally telling signs. You might laugh at jokes you don't find funny, agree with opinions you don't share, or go along with plans you don't enjoy. You may apologize excessively—"Sorry for being late," "Sorry for asking," "Sorry for existing." Each of these is a small way of shrinking yourself, making sure you don't upset the balance.

Another subtle form is over-explaining. When you finally do set a limit, you add long justifications to soften the impact: *I can't come tonight because I have to work, and I'm tired, and I'll make it up to you...* Instead of simply saying no, you try to pad your refusal with reasons, hoping to protect yourself from disapproval. This reveals the underlying fear: that your boundary alone is not valid unless it is wrapped in apology.

The daily cost of these behaviors is that they chip away at authenticity. Each time you go along with something that doesn't feel right, you drift further from yourself. Over time, this creates a sense of emptiness or confusion: *Who am I really, beneath all these yeses?* That question is often what pushes people to finally examine their people-pleasing.

Noticing how the pattern shows up is the first step toward change. It doesn't mean you have to stop being considerate or cooperative. It means pausing to ask whether your choices come from genuine desire or from fear of rejection. A yes rooted in honesty builds connection. A yes rooted in fear builds only resentment. Learning the difference is what turns daily compliance into daily authenticity.

Breaking the Illusion of Approval

One of the strongest forces behind people-pleasing is the belief that approval from others guarantees safety, love, or belonging. It feels reassuring to hear praise, see a smile, or receive validation. For a brief moment, the anxiety quiets. But the relief never lasts, and soon the cycle begins again: another yes, another sacrifice, another attempt to secure acceptance. The illusion is that if you try hard enough, if you never disappoint, approval will finally feel permanent. Yet approval is always temporary, and chasing it keeps you trapped.

The roots of this illusion go back to childhood. When affection or safety depended on compliance, the child's nervous system learned to equate approval with survival. That child may have thought, *If I behave perfectly, I'll be loved. If I never upset anyone, I'll be safe.* Those lessons were carried forward, unchallenged, into adulthood. Now, even in situations where your survival does not depend on compliance, the old belief still drives your choices.

The problem is that approval from others can never fill the deeper need for self-acceptance. External validation is fragile. It changes with moods, circumstances, and other people's unresolved issues. One day you're praised for your hard work, the next you're criticized for not doing enough. One friend admires your generosity, another accuses you of being a pushover. Trying to build a stable sense of worth on such shifting ground is exhausting.

This constant chase also distorts relationships. When your focus is on gaining approval, your interactions stop being authentic. You may say what you think others want to hear rather than what you actually feel. You may hide your struggles to appear strong, or exaggerate your accomplishments to seem impressive. These masks might win temporary admiration, but they prevent real intimacy. People can only connect with the version of you that you present, not with your full self.

Breaking the illusion means realizing that approval is not the same as love. Love can hold space for imperfection, disagreement, even conflict. Approval cannot. It disappears the moment you step out of line. Chasing approval keeps you small because it teaches you to mold yourself into whatever shape will be most pleasing in the moment. Love, on the other hand, allows you to be whole—even messy, even flawed.

This shift begins with noticing the difference between authentic desire and fear-driven compliance. When someone asks something of you, pause before responding. Ask yourself: *Do I genuinely want to do this, or am I afraid of what will happen if I say no?* That pause alone disrupts the automatic reflex to please. Sometimes you'll still choose to say yes, but it will come from choice rather than compulsion. Choice builds trust in yourself; compulsion keeps you dependent on others.

It also helps to test the fear behind disapproval. Often, we imagine catastrophic outcomes: *If I say no, they'll hate me. If I set a boundary, they'll leave me.* But when you experiment with small acts of honesty, you usually find the reaction is less dramatic than you feared. A friend may be disappointed, but they move on. A coworker may grumble, but they adapt. The more you test these moments, the more you realize disapproval is survivable. That realization weakens the illusion.

Another way to break free is to practice self-validation. This doesn't mean pretending you don't care what others think. It means making your own opinion count as much as, or more than, theirs. Start by acknowledging your efforts, your progress, and your feelings without waiting for someone else to recognize them. Write down what you're proud of at the end of the day. Speak to yourself with the same kindness you would use for a child. Over time, this inner approval begins to replace the desperate hunger for outer approval.

Therapy, journaling, or supportive communities can also help in this process. Sometimes the old beliefs are so ingrained that you need guidance to untangle them. Sharing your struggles in a safe space allows you to see that you're not alone, and that your worth does not depend on constant performance. Healing happens in relationships where authenticity is welcomed, not punished.

Breaking the illusion of approval does not mean becoming indifferent to others. Humans are social beings, and feedback will always matter. The difference is that your sense of self no longer rises and falls entirely on other people's opinions. You can listen, consider, and even adjust when appropriate, but you remain rooted in your own truth. Approval becomes information, not a lifeline.

Perhaps the most liberating realization is this: some people will never approve of you, no matter what you do. You can give endlessly, perform flawlessly, and still fall short in their eyes. Recognizing this truth is painful at first, but freeing in the long run. If approval is unattainable for everyone, why sacrifice yourself trying? Redirect that energy toward relationships where love is real and unconditional.

In the end, the illusion of approval collapses when you see that what you were really longing for all along was your own acceptance. Once you begin to offer yourself compassion and care, the grip of external validation loosens. Approval from others can still feel nice, but it no longer dictates your choices. You stop living for applause and start living as yourself. And that, more than any fleeting compliment, is what true safety and belonging feel like.

Chapter 3:
Facing the Inner Critic

Every person carries an inner voice that comments on their actions, decisions, and even their very being. For some, this voice offers gentle guidance. For many, however, it takes the form of a harsh critic— relentless, judgmental, and impossible to satisfy. The inner critic is not an inherent flaw. It is a learned voice, shaped by early experiences, that continues to echo long after childhood has ended. Understanding and facing this critic is essential to healing, because as long as it dominates your inner world, it will silence your inner child and undermine your ability to trust yourself.

The origins of the inner critic can usually be traced back to childhood. Children learn about themselves through the feedback they receive from caregivers, teachers, and peers. When that feedback is supportive, the child internalizes a sense of worth and competence. But when the feedback is consistently critical, dismissive, or shaming, the child absorbs those judgments as truth. Instead of hearing, *You made a mistake,* the child hears, *You are a mistake.* Instead of, *You need to try again,* the message becomes, *You're never good enough.* Over time, these messages become a self-sustaining script, repeating automatically even when the original voices are long gone.

The inner critic often borrows the exact tone and language of authority figures. A parent who constantly demanded excellence leaves behind a voice that berates you for every imperfection. A teacher who shamed you in front of others becomes the echo that tells you you're stupid whenever you struggle. A peer who mocked you becomes the whisper that says you're unlovable whenever you feel vulnerable. Even when you consciously reject those old influences, the critic lingers, because it has been woven into your sense of identity.

At first, the critic may seem useful. It claims to push you toward achievement, discipline, or responsibility. You may even credit it with your successes: *If I weren't so hard on myself, I wouldn't have made it this far.* But the truth is more complicated. The critic motivates through fear, not inspiration. It drives you to avoid failure, shame, or rejection, but it rarely allows you to feel satisfied. Achievements are quickly dismissed—"It wasn't good enough" or "Anyone could have done that." Instead of celebrating growth, the critic moves the finish line further away, ensuring you never truly arrive.

The cost of living under this constant pressure is heavy. The inner critic fuels anxiety, perfectionism, and self-doubt. It keeps you from trying new things because you fear its attack if you fail. It sabotages relationships by convincing you that you're unworthy of love or that others will leave once they see the "real" you. It even erodes physical well-being, because the stress of constant self-judgment wears down the body as much as the mind.

Perhaps the most damaging effect of the critic is the way it silences the inner child. That younger part of you longs for acceptance, play, and freedom to be imperfect. But when the critic dominates, the child is pushed into hiding, terrified of being shamed. You may feel this as a lack of spontaneity or creativity in your adult life. It's not that those qualities don't exist—it's that the critic won't allow them space.

Facing the inner critic does not mean trying to destroy it. Ironically, fighting the critic with more criticism only reinforces its power. The critic developed for a reason: it was a misguided attempt to protect you. As a child, being harsh on yourself might have felt safer than waiting for someone else's judgment. If you punished yourself first, maybe the external punishment would hurt less. Recognizing this protective role doesn't excuse the critic's harm, but it helps you approach it with understanding rather than hatred.

The first step in working with the critic is awareness. Many people live with this inner voice so constantly that they no longer notice it. Start by paying attention to the words running through your mind. When you make a mistake, what do you say to yourself? When you look in the mirror, what's the first thought that arises? Awareness allows you to distinguish between your true self and the critic's commentary.

Once you recognize the critic, you can begin to question it. Ask: *Whose voice does this sound like? When did I first start believing this message? Is it objectively true, or is it just a habit of thought?* Often you'll realize that the critic is simply replaying old scripts that no longer apply. By challenging these automatic messages, you create space for a kinder, more accurate perspective.

Replacing the critic's voice with compassion is the next step. This doesn't mean lying to yourself or ignoring areas for growth. It means speaking to yourself the way you would speak to a child you love. If your inner critic says, *You're worthless,* respond with, *I made a mistake, but that doesn't define me.* If it says, *You'll never succeed,* counter with, *I'm learning, and learning takes time.* These shifts may feel awkward at first, but over time they retrain your inner dialogue.

It's also helpful to externalize the critic. Instead of letting it dominate silently, imagine it as a separate character. Give it a name, a face, even a silly personality. This reduces its authority. When the critic pipes up, you can say, *Thanks for your input, but I don't need that right now.* By creating distance, you remember that the critic is not your whole self—it's just one voice among many, and you have the power to choose which voice to listen to.

Facing the inner critic is not a quick process. It requires patience, consistency, and a willingness to sit with discomfort. But each small act of awareness, questioning, and compassion weakens its grip. Over time, the critic shifts from being a tyrant to a background voice, something you notice but no longer obey. In its place, the inner child begins to reemerge, bringing back curiosity, creativity, and joy.

This chapter marks a turning point in the healing process. By seeing the critic clearly, you stop mistaking it for truth. By responding with compassion, you begin to reclaim your inner world from fear. And by giving the child within you space to exist without judgment, you open the door to trust, freedom, and authenticity. The critic may never disappear entirely, but it no longer has to rule your life.

The Origins of the Inner Critic

The inner critic does not appear out of nowhere. It develops over time, beginning in the earliest years of life, when a child is learning who they are and how the world responds to them. Children depend completely on their caregivers for survival. They look to parents, teachers, and other authority figures not only for food and shelter but also for a sense of worth. Every word of praise or criticism, every gesture of acceptance or rejection, becomes part of the child's understanding of themselves.

When caregivers offer encouragement, the child learns, *I am capable, I am valued.* But when criticism outweighs support, the lesson is very different: *I am never enough. I can't make mistakes. I must earn love by being perfect.* These early lessons sink deep because children lack the perspective to question them. If a parent says, *You're lazy,* the child does not think, *My parent is having a bad day.* They think, *I must really be lazy.* That belief becomes part of identity, and the inner critic takes shape.

The critic often echoes the exact tone and language of authority figures. A parent's harsh words, a teacher's sarcasm, or a peer's mockery can linger for decades, repeating in the adult's mind long after the original voices are gone. Even positive intentions can plant the seeds of a critic. For example, a parent who constantly pushed for excellence may have believed they were motivating their child, but the child internalized the pressure as *I'm never good enough.* The voice of ambition became the voice of self-doubt.

Shame plays a central role in this development. When children are shamed for their natural impulses—crying, needing comfort, making mistakes—they learn that parts of themselves are unacceptable. To avoid future shame, they turn inward, policing their own behavior before anyone else can. The critic becomes the internalized parent, teacher, or peer, ready to punish the child for stepping out of line. What began as an attempt to stay safe turns into a lifelong habit of self-attack.

Cultural and social expectations reinforce this process. Messages about toughness, success, beauty, or obedience shape what children believe they must be. A boy who is told not to cry learns to silence vulnerability. A girl who is praised only for being helpful learns to ignore her own needs. Each unspoken rule adds another layer to the critic's script. By the time the child grows into adulthood, the critic has a full vocabulary of commands, prohibitions, and insults, all aimed at keeping them in line.

It's important to recognize that the critic originally developed as a form of protection. Children who live under constant scrutiny or judgment adapt by internalizing those external voices. In a way, it feels safer to criticize yourself first than to wait for someone else to do it. If you punish yourself quickly enough, maybe others won't notice your mistakes. If you anticipate rejection, maybe you can avoid the pain of being blindsided. This strategy may reduce immediate harm, but it comes at a steep cost: the child learns to fear themselves as much as they fear others.

Understanding these origins changes how we approach the critic today. Instead of seeing it as an enemy to be destroyed, we can view it as a survival mechanism that has outlived its usefulness. The critic once tried to keep you safe in a world that felt unpredictable or unsafe. But now, as an adult, you have resources and choices that the child did not. By seeing the critic through this lens, you can meet it not with hatred but with curiosity.

Tracing the origins of the critic is an act of compassion. It helps you realize that the harsh voice in your head is not proof of your inadequacy—it is proof of how deeply you wanted to be loved and accepted. The critic is the echo of a child's longing for safety. Recognizing that truth is the first step toward loosening its grip, because once you understand where the critic came from, you can begin to decide whether it still deserves to guide your life.

How the Inner Critic Shapes Adult Life

By the time we reach adulthood, the inner critic is often so woven into daily life that it feels like part of our personality. Its words are familiar, its tone almost constant. We may not even notice it anymore—it's simply the background noise that follows us through our days. Yet the critic is far from harmless. Its influence reaches into nearly every area of adult life: work, relationships, health, and, most importantly, the way we relate to ourselves.

One of the clearest places to see the critic's impact is in perfectionism. Adults with a strong inner critic often hold themselves to impossible standards. They strive for flawlessness in their careers, their appearance, or their relationships, driven by the fear that any mistake will expose them as inadequate. On the surface, this drive can look like ambition or discipline. But beneath it lies relentless anxiety. Even when goals are achieved, satisfaction is fleeting. The critic quickly moves the target, insisting that the achievement doesn't count or that it wasn't good enough. The result is a life that looks successful from the outside but feels exhausting from within.

The critic also plays a major role in self-doubt. Many adults second-guess their decisions, replaying scenarios in their heads, searching for reassurance that they did the right thing. This hesitation is not simply caution; it's the critic whispering, *You're going to get it wrong. You can't be trusted.* Over time, this erodes confidence, making it difficult to take risks or pursue new opportunities. Decisions that should be empowering instead become paralyzing.

Relationships are another area deeply shaped by the critic. When the inner voice tells you that you're unlovable, you may cling to others, desperate for reassurance. Or you may push people away, convinced they'll reject you if they get too close. In either case, the critic prevents genuine intimacy. It's hard to let yourself be seen when you believe you are fundamentally flawed. Partners, friends, or colleagues may sense the insecurity, but they can't touch the root of it, because the battle is happening inside your own mind.

The critic's influence also shows up in communication. If you constantly hear, *Don't upset anyone, don't make mistakes, don't show weakness,* you may avoid speaking up even when something matters to you. At work, this might mean staying quiet in meetings, holding back ideas that could make a difference. In personal relationships, it might mean agreeing to things you don't want, just to avoid conflict. The critic convinces you that silence equals safety, but in reality, it leaves you unheard and unfulfilled.

The body does not escape the critic's reach either. Constant self-judgment triggers stress responses, releasing cortisol and other hormones that keep the nervous system on high alert. Over time, this can contribute to anxiety, depression, insomnia, digestive problems, and even cardiovascular issues. The critic is not just a mental voice—it has real physical consequences. Living with constant internal pressure is like running a marathon every day without rest.

Creativity is another casualty. The critic is quick to attack any expression that feels vulnerable: *That idea is stupid. No one will care. Don't embarrass yourself.* Faced with this barrage, many adults stop creating altogether. They avoid painting, writing, singing, or even speaking openly, not because they lack talent, but because the critic convinced them they would fail. The tragedy is that the very qualities that make life rich—play, imagination, curiosity—are silenced before they can emerge.

The critic also interferes with self-care. For some, resting triggers accusations of laziness. For others, setting boundaries sparks feelings of guilt. Even basic needs like food, sleep, and relaxation can become battlegrounds, with the critic insisting that you haven't earned them. This constant pressure to prove your worth by doing more leaves little room for joy or balance. Life becomes about enduring rather than living.

One of the most painful effects of the critic is the way it keeps people stuck in cycles of shame. When you make a mistake, the critic doesn't just point it out—it attacks your entire being: *You're worthless. You'll never get it right.* Shame then fuels more self-criticism, creating a loop that is hard to escape. This loop can become so familiar that you stop questioning it, assuming it's simply the truth about who you are.

The critic is also skilled at undermining progress. Even when you make healthy changes—setting boundaries, practicing self-compassion, trying something new—the critic is quick to dismiss them: *This won't last. You're just fooling yourself. You'll never really change.* By discrediting your efforts, it keeps you tied to old patterns, ensuring that growth feels temporary or impossible.

It's important to note that the critic doesn't always shout. Sometimes it whispers, subtly guiding your choices in ways you don't notice. It might stop you from applying for a job by planting doubt: *You're not qualified.* It might keep you from ending a toxic relationship by insisting: *No one else will want you.* These quiet messages are often more dangerous than the loud attacks, because they feel like reason rather than fear.

Despite all of this, the critic is not invincible. Its power lies in operating unnoticed. Once you start to recognize its presence, you create the possibility of choice. You can begin to ask: *Is this really true, or is it just my critic talking? Do I want to keep living by this voice, or is there another perspective I could listen to?* Awareness doesn't silence the critic overnight, but it creates cracks in its authority.

The truth is that the critic shaped much of your adult life, but it does not have to shape your future. Its voice may always be present, but it does not have to be the voice you obey. By learning to recognize its patterns, question its assumptions, and respond with compassion, you begin to reclaim your freedom. Life under the critic is ruled by fear of failure and rejection. Life beyond the critic is guided by authenticity, courage, and self-acceptance. The difference is not the absence of mistakes, but the presence of kindness toward yourself when mistakes occur.

Recognizing the Critic's Voice

The first step to loosening the grip of the inner critic is learning to notice it. This sounds simple, but many people have lived with the critic for so long that its words feel like truth rather than commentary. You don't think, *My critic is attacking me.* You think, *I really am failing. I really am unworthy.* The critic hides by blending in with your own thoughts.

Start by paying attention to tone. The critic often speaks in absolutes: *always, never, worthless, failure.* It doesn't leave room for nuance. Instead of saying, *You made a mistake on that report,* it says, *You always screw things up.* Instead of, *You were nervous during that meeting,* it says, *You'll never succeed.* The harshness of the language

47

is a giveaway that you're hearing the critic, not your balanced adult self.

Another sign is the speed of the voice. The critic is quick—so quick that it often speaks before you have time to reflect. You drop a glass, and before it hits the floor, the critic is already saying, *You're so clumsy*. You forget a detail, and the critic snaps, *You can't do anything right*. This speed comes from years of rehearsal. The critic doesn't wait to see what really happened; it jumps to the harshest conclusion possible.

Notice also where the voice comes from. Sometimes it echoes the exact words of parents, teachers, or peers from childhood. If you hear, *You'll never amount to anything*, or *Stop being so sensitive*, ask yourself: whose voice is that originally? Tracing it back helps separate it from your identity. What feels like self-criticism is often just an old tape playing on repeat.

The critic is not limited to negative moments. It often undermines success too. You finish a project, and instead of allowing pride, the critic says, *It wasn't that great. Anyone could have done it*. You receive a compliment, and the critic mutters, *They're just being polite*. Recognizing this pattern is crucial because it shows that the critic is not a reliable judge—it attacks regardless of circumstances.

Physical cues can help as well. The critic often stirs up tension in the body: a tight chest, a sinking stomach, clenched jaws. When you feel sudden shame or anxiety without clear cause, pause and ask: *What am I telling myself right now?* More often than not, you'll discover a critical thought running in the background.

Writing can sharpen awareness. Keep a notebook and jot down the critic's words whenever they appear. Seeing them on paper makes them easier to spot and question. It also shows how repetitive they are. Most people discover that their critic relies on a handful of phrases, repeated endlessly. This realization helps reduce their power.

Recognizing the critic's voice is not about silencing every negative thought. It's about learning to distinguish between helpful feedback and destructive attacks. A balanced inner voice might say, *You forgot that deadline—set a reminder next time.* The critic says, *You're hopeless.* The difference is compassion. Once you start to hear the distinction, you can choose which voice to believe.

Responding with Compassion

Recognizing the voice of the inner critic is only half the work. The real change begins when you learn to respond to it differently. Most people instinctively try to silence the critic with more force: *Stop being so harsh, shut up, leave me alone.* But this often backfires. Fighting the critic with aggression simply adds another layer of self-judgment. Instead of feeling relief, you feel trapped in an argument with yourself. What weakens the critic is not more criticism—it is compassion.

Compassion may sound soft, but it is actually a powerful form of strength. It allows you to meet the critic's harshness without collapsing under it and without escalating the conflict. Think of how you would treat a child who made a mistake. You would not scream, *You're worthless.* You would say, *It's okay. Everyone makes mistakes. Let's try again.* Responding to yourself in the same way begins to rewire your inner world.

One simple practice is to pause when the critic speaks and reframe the message. If the critic says, *You're useless,* you can respond, *I'm having a hard moment, but that doesn't define me.* If it says, *You'll never succeed,* counter with, *I'm learning, and learning takes time.* These statements may feel unnatural at first, especially if the critic has been the dominant voice for decades. But every compassionate response weakens the critic's authority and strengthens your capacity for self-trust.

Another approach is to personify the critic. Imagine it as a character—a stern teacher, a relentless boss, or even a cartoon villain. When it speaks, picture it standing outside of you, delivering its lines. Then imagine your compassionate self stepping in, much like a supportive friend would, to say, *Thanks for your input, but I don't need that right now.* This visualization creates distance, reminding you that the critic is not your identity. It's a voice you can choose not to follow.

Compassion also involves offering comfort to the part of you that the critic attacks. Remember that the critic formed to protect a younger version of you from shame or rejection. When it lashes out, it is often the wounded child inside who feels exposed. Instead of battling the critic, turn toward the child. Place a hand on your heart, take a breath, and silently say, *I see you. You are safe with me.* By nurturing the child, you bypass the critic's harshness and give attention to what truly needs care.

Practical self-care reinforces this compassionate stance. Small acts—resting when you're tired, eating when you're hungry, allowing yourself joy without guilt—send the message that your needs matter. Each act contradicts the critic's claim that you don't deserve kindness. Over time, these choices build evidence that you can be trusted to take care of yourself.

Compassionate response also means adjusting expectations. Instead of demanding perfection, allow yourself to be human. If you miss a deadline, rather than spiraling into shame, ask, *What can I learn from this? How can I plan differently next time?* This shift turns mistakes into information instead of weapons. The critic thrives on absolutes—*always, never, failure*—but compassion thrives on perspective.

Support from others can help strengthen this practice. Share your experience with a trusted friend or therapist. Sometimes hearing someone else say, *That sounds harsh—would you ever talk to me that way?* highlights how unreasonable the critic really is. External voices of compassion remind you what kindness sounds like, making it easier to reproduce that tone internally.

Responding with compassion is not about silencing the critic forever. Its voice may never disappear completely. But you don't need it to. The goal is to shift the balance so that the critic no longer controls your choices. When compassion becomes the louder voice, the critic fades into the background—still present, but no longer in charge.

The most important truth is this: compassion is not indulgence. It does not mean lowering your standards or avoiding responsibility. It means creating an environment inside yourself where growth is possible. No one learns well under constant threat of punishment. Children thrive when they feel safe, and the same is true for adults. By meeting yourself with understanding instead of attack, you create the safety that allows real change.

Over time, responding with compassion transforms your inner world. The critic may still whisper, but it no longer dictates your worth. The child within feels safer to come forward, bringing back curiosity, creativity, and joy. And you, the adult, begin to live not under the weight of judgment but in the freedom of acceptance. Compassion is not weakness. It is the strength that allows you to face yourself fully, without fear.

Chapter 4:
Practicing Self-Compassion

For many people, the idea of self-compassion feels uncomfortable, even foreign. We grow up learning how to be polite, generous, and forgiving toward others, but rarely are we taught how to extend the same grace inward. Instead, we often inherit a belief that being hard on ourselves is the only way to improve. If we don't push relentlessly, the inner critic warns, we'll fall apart. Yet research and lived experience show the opposite: people thrive not when they are shamed into change but when they are supported with kindness.

Self-compassion is not indulgence. It does not mean excusing harmful behavior, ignoring responsibility, or living without standards. True self-compassion means treating yourself with the same respect, understanding, and patience that you would naturally offer a friend. When you fail, you comfort instead of punish. When you're tired, you allow rest instead of demanding more. When you feel afraid, you meet yourself with reassurance instead of ridicule.

At its core, self-compassion is built on three elements: mindfulness, common humanity, and kindness. Mindfulness means acknowledging what you feel without exaggerating or suppressing it. Instead of saying, *I shouldn't feel this way,* you simply notice, *I feel sad, I feel anxious, I feel disappointed.* Common humanity is the recognition that you are not alone in your struggles. Every human being fails, doubts, and suffers. Remembering this prevents the critic's trap of isolation—*I'm the only one who can't get it right.* And kindness is the practice of responding to yourself with care. It is the choice to speak in a supportive tone rather than a harsh one, even when you've fallen short.

The challenge is that compassion does not come naturally when the critic has been in charge for years. Many people resist, fearing that if they go easy on themselves, they'll become lazy or careless. But this fear is based on a misunderstanding. Compassion doesn't mean lowering the bar. It means creating the safety that allows you to try, fail, and try again without being crushed by shame. In fact, people who practice self-compassion are more resilient, more motivated, and more consistent in their growth because they are not constantly drained by self-attack.

Practicing self-compassion requires a shift in daily habits. Start with your inner dialogue. Notice the tone you use with yourself, especially in moments of difficulty. If you spill coffee, miss a deadline, or forget an appointment, pay attention to the first words in your head. Are they cruel? Would you ever speak that way to someone you care about? The practice is to replace those harsh words with gentler ones—not to pretend nothing happened, but to remind yourself that mistakes are part of being human.

Physical gestures can support this shift. Placing a hand on your chest, taking a slow breath, or quietly saying, *I'm here for you,* may feel awkward at first, but the body responds to signals of care. Just as a child calms when held, your nervous system relaxes when you offer yourself comfort. Over time, these small acts retrain your body to associate difficulty not with attack but with support.

Compassion also means honoring your limits. This includes saying no when you are overextended, resting when you are exhausted, and allowing yourself pleasure without guilt. Many people equate self-care with selfishness, but compassion recognizes it as necessity. Just as you cannot pour from an empty cup, you cannot live authentically while ignoring your own needs. Each act of honoring your limits reinforces the message that your well-being matters.

Another way to practice compassion is through reflection. Try journaling about a recent mistake or difficult moment. Instead of analyzing what went wrong, write to yourself as if you were writing to a dear friend. Offer understanding, reassurance, and perspective. This exercise may feel strange at first, but it helps you experience what compassion sounds like in your own voice. With repetition, that voice becomes easier to access in daily life.

Self-compassion also means challenging cultural myths. Many societies prize toughness, productivity, and self-sacrifice, while dismissing gentleness as weakness. But ask yourself: has relentless self-criticism made you stronger, or has it left you exhausted? True strength lies in flexibility, not rigidity. It takes courage to soften in a world that constantly tells you to harden. Choosing compassion is not avoiding life's challenges—it is equipping yourself to face them without collapsing.

Relationships benefit as well. When you stop attacking yourself, you have more patience and kindness to offer others. You no longer depend on them to fill the gaps left by your self-criticism, nor do you resent them for seeing your flaws. Compassion creates space for authenticity, because you are no longer hiding behind the fear of being judged. Ironically, by being gentler with yourself, you become stronger in your connections with others.

The practice of self-compassion is not a quick fix. It requires patience, especially if your critic has been loud for decades. At first, compassionate words may feel hollow. You may even hear the critic mock you for trying: *This is silly. You'll never change.* But persistence matters. Each time you choose kindness over cruelty, you strengthen a new pathway in your mind. Gradually, the compassionate voice grows louder, and the critic grows weaker.

Ultimately, self-compassion is about reclaiming your humanity. It is about remembering that worth is not something to be earned through perfection or performance. It is already yours, by virtue of being alive. The child inside you has waited for this truth for a long time. By practicing compassion, you offer that child what they needed most: acceptance without condition.

This chapter marks a shift from awareness to practice. The earlier chapters helped you recognize the inner child, people-pleasing patterns, and the critic's voice. Now, self-compassion becomes the tool that allows healing to take root. Without it, the work feels like another demand, another way to prove yourself. With it, the work becomes sustainable, even nourishing. Compassion is the soil in which all other changes can grow.

What Self-Compassion Really Means

When people first hear the phrase "self-compassion," they often confuse it with self-indulgence. They imagine letting themselves off the hook, ignoring responsibilities, or making excuses. But true self-compassion has nothing to do with avoiding growth. It is about creating the inner conditions where growth can happen without shame.

At its core, self-compassion is treating yourself the way you would treat a close friend. If a friend came to you after making a mistake, you wouldn't say, *You're pathetic. You'll never get it right.* You would say, *That was tough, but it doesn't define you. You can try again.* Self-compassion is offering yourself the same understanding. It means refusing to speak to yourself in a way you would never dream of speaking to someone you love.

There are three main elements to this practice. The first is mindfulness—acknowledging what you feel without denying or exaggerating it. Instead of burying sadness or turning disappointment into catastrophe, you simply recognize, *This hurts.* That honesty alone creates space for healing.

The second is common humanity—the recognition that you are not alone in your struggles. Everyone fails, everyone doubts, everyone suffers. When you remember that imperfection is universal, the shame of "I'm the only one" begins to dissolve.

The third is kindness—the willingness to respond to your pain with care. Kindness might sound like gentle words: *I'm proud of you for trying.* It might look like resting when you're tired or allowing yourself joy without guilt. Whatever form it takes, kindness is the opposite of the harshness that the inner critic thrives on.

Understanding self-compassion in this way reveals that it is not weakness but strength. It doesn't mean lowering your standards. It means giving yourself the resilience to keep going after setbacks, to learn without fear, and to grow without constant self-attack.

Overcoming Resistance to Kindness

For many people, the hardest part of self-compassion is not understanding what it means but allowing themselves to practice it. Even when they see the damage caused by relentless self-criticism, a quiet voice inside says, *If I stop being hard on myself, I'll fall apart.* This resistance runs deep, rooted in childhood lessons, cultural values, and years of repetition. To build a compassionate relationship with yourself, you must first face and dismantle the barriers that make kindness feel dangerous.

One common barrier is the belief that self-compassion equals weakness. Many of us were raised in environments that praised toughness and ridiculed softness. Crying was a sign of being "too sensitive." Admitting fear or sadness was labeled dramatic. In that atmosphere, the critic felt like an ally—it pushed you to toughen up, to keep going, to hide what was vulnerable. As an adult, those old messages can make gentleness feel suspicious, as if kindness will make you soft and unprepared. The truth, though, is that compassion doesn't remove resilience; it fuels it. People who treat themselves with patience bounce back from setbacks faster than those who attack themselves, because shame drains energy while compassion restores it.

Another barrier is the fear of becoming lazy or complacent. The critic insists, *If you don't push yourself harder, you'll never succeed.* This is a convincing lie because it borrows from past experiences where fear of failure drove achievement. But achievement motivated by fear rarely brings lasting satisfaction. It keeps you running, never resting, always looking over your shoulder. Self-compassion shifts the motivation from fear to care. When you pursue goals because you value yourself, not because you're terrified of failing, the energy becomes steadier, more sustainable.

Some people resist compassion because they confuse it with self-pity. They imagine that if they are gentle with themselves, they will wallow in problems instead of solving them. But compassion is not about sinking deeper into pain; it's about offering enough safety that you can face pain without being crushed by it. Self-pity isolates—*No one has it as bad as me.* Compassion connects—*Struggle is part of being human, and I'm not alone in this.* One keeps you stuck; the other helps you move forward.

Another form of resistance comes from shame itself. When you've carried the belief for years that you are unworthy, kindness can feel unbearable. The critic whispers, *You don't deserve compassion. If people knew the real you, they'd reject you.* This is one of the cruelest tricks of shame: it convinces you that the very thing you most need— acceptance—is the one thing you cannot have. The way through is to start small. Offer yourself tiny acts of care, even when they feel undeserved. Over time, these acts prove to the wounded child inside that love does not have to be earned.

Cultural myths reinforce this resistance. Productivity is often valued above well-being. People are praised for overwork, for ignoring their needs, for sacrificing themselves. In such a culture, choosing rest or gentleness can feel rebellious. You may even fear judgment from others: *If I slow down, people will think I'm weak. If I say no, they'll think I'm selfish.* But compassion is not selfish—it's necessary. Without it, you burn out, resent others, and lose the ability to give authentically. With it, you maintain the energy and honesty that sustain healthy relationships.

One practical way to work through resistance is to experiment with what compassion actually feels like. Instead of trying to convince yourself with logic, try small practices: place a hand on your chest when you're upset, whisper a kind phrase to yourself, or allow yourself an extra hour of rest when you're tired. Notice how your body responds. Often, the nervous system relaxes almost immediately, proving that kindness is not weakness but medicine.

It also helps to reflect on how you treat others. Think about how you respond when a loved one struggles. Do you berate them? Or do you offer encouragement and patience? If you can extend compassion outward, you already know how to do it. The challenge is turning that same tone inward. When resistance rises, ask yourself: *Why do I believe others deserve kindness but not me?* That question alone can expose the double standard the critic has imposed.

Therapeutic support or safe relationships can help dismantle resistance too. Sometimes, the first experience of true compassion comes from outside—through a therapist's validation, a partner's patience, or a friend's empathy. These experiences model what self-compassion can sound like, giving you a template to internalize. Over time, the external support becomes an internal voice, something you can offer yourself even when no one else is around.

It's also important to acknowledge that resistance is normal. If self-compassion feels foreign or even threatening, it doesn't mean you're incapable of it. It means you learned different survival skills and are now being asked to try a new one. Like any new skill, it will feel awkward at first. The critic may even mock you for trying: *This is silly. You'll never change.* But awkwardness is not proof of failure—it's proof of learning.

Overcoming resistance is not about eliminating doubt completely. It's about practicing compassion anyway, even when the critic argues against it. Each time you choose kindness in the face of resistance, you weaken the old belief that harshness is the only path to success. With repetition, compassion becomes less foreign and more natural, until it feels less like rebellion and more like home.

Daily Practices for a Kinder Inner Voice

Self-compassion is not a single decision but a practice built moment by moment. Just like any habit, it strengthens with repetition. The more often you choose kindness over harshness, the more natural it becomes to meet yourself with care. Building a kinder inner voice requires practical tools—simple, everyday actions that gradually replace the critic's script with a tone of support.

One of the most powerful practices is mindful self-talk. This means becoming aware of the running commentary in your mind and deliberately shifting its tone. When you notice the critic saying, *You blew it again,* pause and ask yourself how you would respond if a friend were in the same situation. You might say, *You tried your best. Everyone makes mistakes. What can we do differently next time?* Then repeat those words to yourself. At first, this feels forced, but over time the brain begins to adopt the new script as default.

Another daily tool is the use of compassionate phrases or mantras. Choose a few short sentences that comfort you, such as: *I am doing the best I can. I deserve kindness. I am not alone in this.* Write them on sticky notes and place them where you'll see them—on your mirror, your desk, your phone screen. When stress rises, repeat them out loud or silently. These phrases act as anchors, reminding you that you have another option besides self-attack.

Journaling is also effective for reshaping the inner voice. Set aside a few minutes each evening to reflect on the day. Instead of listing everything you did wrong, write about one thing you handled well or one moment when you showed resilience. If you struggled, write to yourself as if you were comforting a younger version of you. *I know today was hard. You felt overwhelmed, but you kept going. I'm proud of you.* Putting compassionate words on paper makes them more concrete and easier to believe.

Self-compassion can be practiced through the body too. When the critic is loud, physical gestures can calm the nervous system. Place a hand on your chest, take three slow breaths, or wrap your arms around yourself in a gentle hug. These actions may seem small, but they send signals of safety to your body. Over time, your body begins to associate difficult moments not with attack but with comfort, making it easier to respond with compassion automatically.

Another practice is setting micro-boundaries during the day. Notice when you feel the pull to overextend—agreeing to one more task, staying up too late, ignoring hunger. Instead of pushing through, experiment with a small act of self-respect. Say no to the extra task. Go to bed on time. Eat when you're hungry. These everyday choices communicate to your inner voice that your needs matter. The critic thrives on self-neglect; boundaries teach it that care is non-negotiable.

Mindfulness exercises help quiet the critic's chatter. Spend five minutes focusing on your breath, noticing thoughts as they arise. When the critic interrupts, label the thought: *That's self-judgment.* Then return your focus to the breath. This labeling weakens the critic's authority by showing that its words are just thoughts, not absolute truths. With practice, you begin to recognize criticism as background noise rather than commands you must obey.

Compassion can also be built through play and joy. Many adults forget that laughter and creativity are forms of self-care. Try coloring, dancing to music, or taking a walk simply to notice the sky. These activities feed the inner child and remind the critic that life is not just about performance. When you create space for joy, the inner voice naturally softens, because you're proving that worth is not tied only to achievement.

It's important to keep expectations realistic. A kinder inner voice will not appear overnight. Some days, the critic will be louder than others. Progress may feel uneven. That's normal. The practice is not about perfection but persistence. Each time you interrupt a harsh thought with a gentler one, you are strengthening new mental pathways. Even if it feels awkward or incomplete, it counts.

Daily practices for self-compassion are less about grand gestures and more about consistent reminders. Every sticky note, every pause, every gentle breath is a step toward rewriting your inner dialogue. Over weeks and months, these steps add up. The critic may still whisper, but the kinder voice grows louder, offering reassurance instead of attack. That shift changes not only how you treat yourself but how you show up in every part of your life.

Living with Compassionate Boundaries

One of the clearest signs that self-compassion has taken root is the ability to set and maintain boundaries. For people who have spent years people-pleasing or silencing their needs, boundaries often feel uncomfortable, even frightening. Saying no can trigger guilt. Asking for space can feel selfish. Yet boundaries are not walls that push people away—they are expressions of respect for both yourself and others. When grounded in compassion, they create healthier relationships and protect your energy without shutting down your heart.

A boundary begins with recognizing your own limits. Your body and emotions often signal when a line is being crossed. Maybe you feel a knot in your stomach when a colleague asks you to take on more work. Maybe you feel drained after spending time with a friend who only takes and never gives. The critic may try to override these signals— *Don't make a fuss, just deal with it*—but compassion listens closely. It says, *Your feelings are information. Your limits matter.*

Living with compassionate boundaries means giving yourself permission to honor those signals. Instead of automatically saying yes, you pause and ask, *What do I truly want? What do I need to stay healthy and present?* Sometimes the answer is yes, sometimes no. The difference is that your decision comes from care rather than fear. You're not pleasing others to avoid rejection; you're choosing honestly, knowing that authenticity sustains real connection.

Boundaries also reshape how you give. When you say yes out of guilt or compulsion, resentment builds. But when you say yes because you genuinely want to, your giving is lighter, freer, more sustainable. Compassionate boundaries don't make you less generous—they make your generosity real. They ensure that what you offer is a gift, not an obligation.

It's natural to fear others' reactions when you start setting boundaries. Some people may be surprised or even upset, especially if they've grown used to your constant compliance. But their discomfort doesn't mean you're wrong. It simply reveals that the relationship was built on an unspoken expectation that you would always sacrifice. Compassion helps you navigate this moment by reminding you: *I'm not rejecting them; I'm respecting myself.* Over time, relationships that can adapt to your honesty become stronger, while those that can't may fade. Both outcomes serve your well-being.

Practical language makes boundaries easier to express. Short, direct statements work best: *I can't take that on right now. I need some time to rest. That doesn't work for me.* Notice how these phrases are clear but not cruel. Compassion is built into the tone—they respect the other person while also respecting you. Practicing these sentences in low-stakes situations, like declining an extra task at work or saying no to an invitation, builds confidence for more challenging moments.

Self-compassion also helps when guilt inevitably shows up. The critic may tell you that you're selfish or unkind. In those moments, remind yourself: *Taking care of myself is not selfish; it's necessary.* Repeat it until your body begins to believe it. Each time you hold a boundary despite guilt, you strengthen the message to your inner child: *Your needs matter too.*

Boundaries are not only about saying no—they're also about saying yes to what nourishes you. Yes to rest, yes to play, yes to relationships where you feel seen. When you build a life shaped by compassionate choices, you create an environment where the inner child can thrive. Safety no longer comes from pleasing others but from trusting yourself to honor what feels right.

Living with compassionate boundaries is not about perfection. You will sometimes overextend or agree when you wish you hadn't. That's part of learning. The key is to notice, reflect, and adjust without shame. Each misstep becomes practice in self-awareness, another chance to remind yourself that growth is ongoing.

In the end, boundaries are acts of love. They protect your energy so you can show up authentically in the world. They teach others how to treat you by modeling respect. And they prove to the critic, again and again, that compassion is not weakness. It is strength—the kind of strength that allows you to stay open, connected, and true to yourself without being consumed.

Chapter 5:
Understanding Healthy Boundaries

Boundaries are one of the most misunderstood aspects of emotional well-being. Many people hear the word and immediately think of walls, rejection, or selfishness. They worry that setting boundaries means pushing others away or becoming cold and detached. But healthy boundaries are the opposite of distance—they are the structures that allow closeness to thrive without fear of losing yourself. Without them, relationships become blurred, imbalanced, and unsustainable. With them, connection becomes safer, clearer, and more authentic.

A boundary is simply the recognition of where you end and where another person begins. It is an acknowledgment that your thoughts, feelings, body, and time are your own, just as others' are theirs. This recognition is what allows two people to meet as equals, each responsible for their own needs and respectful of the other's. Without boundaries, one person's needs consume the relationship while the other's are silenced. With boundaries, both people have space to be themselves.

The difficulty is that many of us were never taught to see boundaries as healthy. As children, we may have been told to hug relatives even when we didn't want to, to share toys even when we weren't ready, or to stay silent about feelings that made adults uncomfortable. These lessons taught us that our needs were less important than compliance. By the time we reached adulthood, saying no felt dangerous, and expressing discomfort felt rude. The critic reinforced these lessons, whispering that protecting yourself meant hurting others.

Yet boundaries are not acts of harm—they are acts of clarity. When you set a boundary, you are not rejecting the other person; you are defining the terms of respectful connection. Imagine a house with no doors or walls. Anyone could walk in, rearrange the furniture, and use the space however they wanted. You would feel unsafe and resentful. Now imagine a house with locked gates and no entry at all. That would feel isolating and lonely. A healthy house has doors and windows: ways for people to come in, but only when invited. Boundaries are the doors and windows of relationships.

One of the reasons boundaries feel so difficult is the fear of others' reactions. If you say no to a request, will the person be angry? If you ask for space, will they leave? These fears are understandable, especially if you grew up in environments where expressing needs led to conflict or punishment. But the truth is that boundaries reveal the quality of relationships. People who value you will respect your limits, even if they feel disappointed. People who only value what you provide may resist or withdraw. In either case, you gain clarity: boundaries show you who is capable of genuine connection and who is not.

Boundaries also prevent resentment. When you agree to things out of guilt or fear, you may appear generous on the surface, but inside frustration builds. Over time, this quiet resentment poisons the relationship far more than an honest no ever could. By setting boundaries early and consistently, you keep relationships clean. You give others the chance to know the real you—not the version that sacrifices silently, but the one who engages authentically.

There are many forms of boundaries. Physical boundaries involve your body and personal space. Emotional boundaries involve your feelings and the responsibility for managing them. Time boundaries involve how you spend your hours and energy. Intellectual boundaries involve your right to your own opinions and beliefs. In each area, clarity allows for respect. For example, telling a coworker, *I can't stay late tonight,* is a time boundary. Saying to a friend, *I'm not comfortable talking about that subject right now,* is an emotional boundary. Neither is cruel—they are simply clear statements of where your line is.

Healthy boundaries also work inwardly. They are not only about what you tell others but also about how you treat yourself. When you push through exhaustion without rest, you cross your own physical boundary. When you overload your schedule, you cross your own time boundary. Self-compassion requires internal boundaries—the discipline to say no not only to others but also to the critic inside that demands endless output.

The process of building boundaries takes practice. Start small. Choose one area of your life where you often feel overextended, and experiment with saying no. Expect discomfort; guilt will almost certainly rise at first. But remind yourself that guilt is not proof of wrongdoing. It is simply the echo of old conditioning. With repetition, the discomfort fades, and confidence grows.

It helps to use clear, simple language. Boundaries don't need lengthy explanations or apologies. Phrases like, *I can't commit to that right now,* or *That doesn't work for me,* are often enough. The more directly you communicate, the less room there is for misunderstanding. If someone presses, you can repeat yourself calmly, like a broken record, without adding justification. This shows that your boundary is firm but not hostile.

Over time, living with boundaries transforms not just relationships but also your sense of self. Each time you set a limit, you reinforce the message to your inner child: *Your needs matter. Your voice deserves to be heard.* The critic may argue that you are selfish or unkind, but your lived experience proves otherwise. You begin to see that boundaries don't reduce love—they deepen it, because they make love safer.

Ultimately, boundaries are acts of trust. They say: *I trust myself to know what I need, and I trust others to handle the truth of who I am.* Not everyone will respond well, but those who do are the ones worth keeping close. Healthy boundaries are not barriers to intimacy. They are the foundation that makes intimacy possible, because without them, connection is built on fear and pretense. With them, connection is built on honesty and respect.

Why Boundaries Are Essential

Boundaries are often misunderstood. Many people associate them with selfishness or distance, as if drawing a line automatically means rejecting others. But healthy boundaries are not about shutting people out. They are about creating conditions where connection can be safe and sustainable. Without boundaries, relationships quickly become imbalanced, leaving one person drained and the other unaware of the cost.

At their core, boundaries are about respect—respect for yourself and respect for others. When you recognize your own limits, you prevent resentment from building in silence. When you respect someone else's limits, you show that you value their autonomy as much as your own. In this way, boundaries make intimacy possible. Without them, connection is built on compliance rather than authenticity.

Consider how this plays out in everyday life. A person who never says no at work eventually burns out, resenting colleagues who continue to ask for help. A partner who always gives in during disagreements eventually feels invisible, wondering if their needs will ever matter. A parent who never carves out rest eventually feels overwhelmed, unable to show up fully for their children. Each of these situations could be prevented by clear, compassionate boundaries.

Boundaries also protect energy. Every yes you give consumes time, attention, and emotional space. When you say yes automatically, you may end up giving away resources you don't have. Boundaries allow you to pause and ask: *Do I truly want to give here? Do I have the energy to do so?* This pause ensures that your yes carries meaning. It also ensures that when you do give, it comes from a place of choice rather than compulsion.

Perhaps the most important reason boundaries are essential is the message they send to your inner child. Each time you set a limit, you remind that younger part of you that their needs matter too. You prove that safety does not require erasing yourself. Over time, this practice heals the old belief that love must be earned through sacrifice. Boundaries say: *I am worthy of care, and I can protect myself while still connecting with others.*

Healthy boundaries are not barriers to closeness—they are the very structures that make closeness possible. By defining where you end and another begins, you create space for mutual respect. You no longer give out of fear or guilt, and you no longer accept what harms you. Instead, you relate from a place of honesty. That honesty may feel uncomfortable at first, but it is the soil where trust grows.

Different Types of Boundaries

When people first hear the word *boundaries*, they often picture saying no to a request or refusing an invitation. While that is one form, boundaries are far more varied and nuanced. They shape every part of how we relate—to our bodies, our emotions, our time, our beliefs, and even to ourselves. Understanding the different types of boundaries makes it easier to recognize where yours may be missing and where they need strengthening.

Physical Boundaries

Physical boundaries involve your body, space, and comfort with touch. These are often the first boundaries we encounter as children, though many of us were taught to ignore them. Being told to hug a relative when you didn't want to or being scolded for saying no to touch taught you that your physical comfort wasn't important. As adults, physical boundaries might include saying, *I'm not comfortable shaking hands right now*, or, *I need personal space*. Respecting these boundaries protects your sense of safety and control over your own body.

Emotional Boundaries

Emotional boundaries protect your feelings and your responsibility for them. Without them, you may take on other people's moods as your own, or you may allow others to dismiss or invalidate your emotions. Healthy emotional boundaries sound like: *I understand you're upset, but I need to step away right now*, or *I hear your opinion, but I feel differently*. These boundaries remind you that while empathy matters, you are not required to absorb everyone else's emotions.

Time Boundaries

Time is one of our most precious resources, yet many people struggle to protect it. Without time boundaries, you may find yourself overloaded with commitments, saying yes to everything while neglecting rest or priorities. Time boundaries involve being clear about how you spend your hours. They might include leaving work at a reasonable time, setting limits on social media, or declining an invitation because you need downtime. Each of these protects your energy and ensures your life reflects what matters most to you.

Intellectual Boundaries

Intellectual boundaries involve your right to your own thoughts, opinions, and ideas. Without them, you may feel silenced in conversations or pressured to agree with beliefs you don't share. Respecting intellectual boundaries means acknowledging differences without attacking or dismissing. You might say, *I see this differently, but I respect your view,* or, *I'd prefer not to debate this right now.* These boundaries encourage curiosity and respect while protecting your mental space.

Material Boundaries

Material boundaries involve how you handle possessions and finances. If you struggle with this area, you may find yourself lending money you can't afford to lose or feeling obligated to share items you'd rather not. Healthy material boundaries sound like, *I can't lend money right now,* or, *I'd rather not share my car.* Setting these limits prevents resentment and ensures that generosity comes from willingness, not pressure.

Internal Boundaries

Perhaps the most overlooked type are internal boundaries—the limits you set with yourself. These involve managing your own impulses, thoughts, and choices. Without internal boundaries, you may overwork, overindulge, or ignore your body's signals. Internal boundaries sound like, *I've done enough for today, it's time to rest,* or, *I won't let my critic dictate this decision.* They are acts of self-discipline rooted not in punishment but in self-respect.

Why Variety Matters

Recognizing these different forms of boundaries highlights how much they affect daily life. You might be firm with time but loose with emotions, or strong with physical space but weak with self-discipline. Each area influences the others. For example, if you lack time boundaries, exhaustion may weaken your emotional boundaries, making you more likely to absorb others' moods. Building awareness across all types helps you identify the areas where you are most vulnerable to burnout or resentment.

Boundaries are not about rigidity. They are about clarity. They can shift depending on context. You might allow close friends into emotional spaces you would not share with acquaintances. You might lend money to a sibling but not to a coworker. The key is that these choices are yours, not forced by fear or guilt.

What unites all boundaries—physical, emotional, time, intellectual, material, and internal—is the message they send: *I respect myself, and I expect respect in return.* Without them, relationships drift into imbalance. With them, connection becomes more honest and sustainable. Boundaries are not about closing doors; they are about choosing which doors to open and when.

Overcoming the Guilt of Saying No

For many people, the hardest part of setting boundaries is not deciding what they want but dealing with the guilt that follows. The simple act of saying no can trigger a wave of self-doubt: *Am I being selfish? Am I letting someone down? What if they get angry?* These feelings are powerful because they are rooted in old survival strategies. Learning to manage them is what allows you to build boundaries that last.

Guilt around boundaries usually comes from childhood lessons. If you were praised for being "the good kid" who never caused trouble, you likely absorbed the belief that your worth came from compliance. If you were scolded for saying no or punished for expressing needs, you may have learned that boundaries equal rejection. Even as an adult, those lessons echo through your nervous system. Saying no feels like a threat to connection, even when logic tells you otherwise.

Another source of guilt is cultural conditioning. Many societies prize self-sacrifice and productivity. People who give endlessly are admired, while those who protect their time are criticized as lazy or selfish. Under this lens, saying no feels like breaking an unspoken rule: always be available, always give more. But these cultural myths ignore a basic truth: no one can give endlessly without breaking down. Real generosity requires sustainability, and sustainability requires boundaries.

The key to overcoming guilt is reframing what no actually means. No is not a rejection of the other person—it is an affirmation of your own limits. It does not say, *I don't care about you.* It says, *I also care about myself.* This perspective shifts the narrative from selfishness to balance. By protecting your energy, you ensure that when you do say yes, it comes from honesty rather than resentment.

Practical strategies can help in this process. Start by practicing no in low-stakes situations. Decline a small invitation, ask for more time before committing, or let someone know you can't take on an extra task. Notice the feelings that arise—guilt, anxiety, fear—and breathe through them. With repetition, your nervous system begins to learn that saying no is survivable. The feared rejection often doesn't come, and even when it does, you realize you can handle it.

It also helps to prepare simple language for boundaries. Many people over-explain or justify their no, as if piling on reasons will protect them from disapproval. In reality, explanations often invite debate. Clear, short phrases work best: *I can't do that right now. That doesn't work for me. I need to rest this evening.* These statements are respectful but firm. They show that your decision is not open to negotiation.

When guilt rises, remind yourself that it is just an echo of old conditioning, not proof of wrongdoing. Place a hand on your heart and silently repeat: *It's okay to protect my energy. My needs matter too.* This physical and verbal reassurance helps calm the nervous system and reinforces new beliefs. Over time, guilt softens and is replaced by confidence.

Support from others can also ease the process. Share your experiences with trusted friends or a therapist who can remind you that boundaries are healthy. Sometimes hearing someone else say, *Of course you deserve to say no,* provides the external validation you need until your inner voice grows stronger.

The truth is, guilt is not a signal that you've done something wrong. It is simply a sign that you are stepping outside old patterns. Every time you set a boundary despite guilt, you retrain your mind and body to associate no not with danger but with self-respect. Slowly, the fear of rejection gives way to the relief of authenticity.

Overcoming guilt is not about eliminating it entirely. It may always show up in small ways. The difference is that it no longer controls your choices. You can feel guilt, acknowledge it, and still honor your limits. That is what freedom looks like: acting from truth rather than fear.

Communicating Boundaries with Clarity and Respect

Setting boundaries in your mind is one thing. Communicating them out loud is another—and often the part that feels most intimidating. Many people know what they want to say but stumble when the moment comes. They worry about sounding rude, hurting someone's feelings, or being misunderstood. Yet boundaries only work when they are expressed clearly. Silence leaves room for assumptions, and assumptions usually lead to disappointment or resentment.

The first principle of healthy communication is clarity. Boundaries lose their power when they are vague. Saying, *Maybe I'll help if I have time,* leaves the door open for pressure. Saying, *I won't be able to help with that project,* is direct and leaves no doubt. Clarity may feel blunt at first, especially if you are used to softening your words, but in reality, it is a kindness. It prevents confusion and allows others to adjust their expectations without guessing.

Respect is the second principle. Boundaries are not weapons; they are guidelines for connection. You don't need to raise your voice or justify yourself endlessly. A calm, steady tone communicates that your decision is firm but not hostile. For example: *I'm not available this weekend, but I hope it goes well*, or *I can't lend money, but I care about your situation*. The words are clear, yet the tone keeps the door open for relationship.

It also helps to prepare language in advance. Many people panic in the moment and end up backtracking or over-explaining. Practicing simple phrases gives you confidence:

- *That doesn't work for me.*
- *I need some time to myself tonight.*
- *I can't commit to that right now.*

These short sentences are respectful, and repetition makes them easier to use when pressure rises.

Another helpful strategy is the "broken record" technique. When someone pushes back, you don't need to invent new reasons each time. You can calmly repeat the same phrase: *I understand, but I'm not available. I hear you, but my answer is still no.* Over-explaining often invites debate, while steady repetition communicates that your boundary is not negotiable.

It's also important to remember that how someone reacts to your boundary is about them, not about you. Some people will be disappointed or even upset. That doesn't mean you were wrong to set the limit. It means the relationship is adjusting to new terms. Compassion helps here. You can acknowledge their feelings without abandoning your boundary: *I know this is frustrating, and I still need to say no.* This blend of empathy and firmness shows respect for both sides.

Timing matters too. Whenever possible, communicate boundaries early, before resentment builds. If you know you can't take on more work, say so before deadlines pile up. If you need space in a relationship, bring it up before frustration explodes. Early communication reduces conflict and gives others time to adapt.

Nonverbal cues also play a role. Your body language and tone often communicate more than your words. A shaky voice or apologetic posture can suggest uncertainty, encouraging others to push. A steady tone, eye contact, and relaxed posture reinforce your message. Practicing these cues in safe environments, like with a friend or therapist, can help you build confidence for harder conversations.

Compassionate boundary-setting is not about being rigid. Flexibility has its place. Sometimes you may choose to stretch a boundary for someone you care about, knowing it won't harm you. The key is that the choice is yours, not driven by guilt or fear. Healthy flexibility feels empowering, while unhealthy compromise feels draining.

Over time, communicating boundaries becomes less about rehearsing phrases and more about embodying a new way of relating. You begin to trust that your needs are valid and that expressing them is an act of respect, not selfishness. Relationships that can handle honesty grow stronger, while those that cannot may fall away. Either way, you gain clarity and peace.

The more you practice, the more natural it feels. At first, you may leave conversations replaying every word, worrying if you sounded harsh. With time, those doubts fade. You learn that clarity and respect can coexist, that no is not rejection, and that true connection only thrives where truth is welcome.

Boundaries communicated with clarity and respect are not barriers. They are bridges—structures that allow you to stay connected without losing yourself. They show others how to treat you and show yourself that your voice deserves to be heard. And with each conversation, you reinforce the most important boundary of all: the commitment to honor your own worth.

Chapter 6:
Building Emotional Awareness

Many of us grow up learning to mistrust or ignore our emotions. We are told not to cry, not to get angry, not to be "too sensitive." In school and at home, logic and achievement are praised, while feelings are treated as distractions. By adulthood, countless people can describe what they think but struggle to describe what they feel. This disconnection leaves them vulnerable to stress, resentment, and patterns of people-pleasing that never seem to end. Building emotional awareness is the process of reversing that conditioning—of learning to recognize, name, and understand your feelings so that they can guide you instead of overwhelm you.

Emotions are not enemies. They are signals, much like physical sensations. Just as pain in your hand tells you to pull away from a hot stove, sadness may signal loss, anger may signal injustice, and anxiety may signal threat. When you ignore these signals, you lose access to important information. When you pay attention, you gain clarity about your needs and boundaries. Emotional awareness is less about controlling how you feel and more about listening to what your feelings are trying to tell you.

One of the challenges in developing awareness is that emotions often arrive in disguise. Anger may mask fear. Irritability may mask exhaustion. Numbness may mask grief. The critic adds another layer by dismissing or shaming emotions before you can even acknowledge them: *Stop being dramatic. You shouldn't feel that way. Get over it.* Over time, you may learn to cut off emotions before they fully register, leaving you confused or disconnected.

Rebuilding awareness begins with slowing down. Instead of rushing past discomfort, pause and notice what is happening in your body.

Tight shoulders, a racing heart, or a heavy chest are clues that emotions are present. Ask yourself: *What am I feeling right now?* At first, the answer may be vague—*bad, stressed, off*. With practice, you begin to identify more precise emotions: *I feel anxious because I'm afraid of disappointing someone. I feel angry because my boundary was crossed. I feel sad because something I hoped for didn't happen.* Naming emotions accurately is the foundation of awareness.

Emotional awareness also involves recognizing intensity. A mild annoyance is different from deep rage. A passing sadness is different from profound grief. Learning to gauge intensity helps you respond appropriately. You don't need the same strategy for a flicker of irritation as you do for overwhelming despair. By tuning in, you can match your coping skills to the size of the emotion.

Another aspect of awareness is connecting emotions to triggers. When you feel upset, ask: *What just happened? What story am I telling myself about this?* Often, the trigger is not only the event but the meaning attached to it. A friend canceling plans may trigger disappointment, but the deeper story might be, *I'm not important.* By noticing the link between event, story, and feeling, you begin to separate the present from old wounds. This clarity reduces the critic's power and gives you more choice in how to respond.

Journaling can be a powerful tool for building awareness. Writing about your day with a focus on emotions—not just events—helps you identify patterns. Over time, you may notice that certain situations consistently trigger anxiety, or that certain people consistently leave you drained. These insights are invaluable for setting boundaries and making choices that protect your well-being.

Mindfulness practices also support emotional awareness. Sitting quietly, focusing on your breath, and noticing thoughts and sensations without judgment helps you stay present with feelings instead of avoiding them. Even a few minutes a day can train your brain to observe emotions without immediately reacting or suppressing them. This space between feeling and action is where freedom lives.

Developing emotional awareness does not mean drowning in feelings. It means finding balance. Some people fear that if they let themselves feel sadness, they'll never stop crying. Or if they acknowledge anger, they'll lose control. But the opposite is usually true. Emotions that are acknowledged tend to pass more quickly, while emotions that are suppressed often linger or resurface in unhealthy ways. Awareness is the difference between carrying a backpack of unacknowledged weight and opening it to see what's inside. Once you know what you're carrying, you can decide what to keep and what to set down.

Emotional awareness also strengthens relationships. When you can name and express what you feel, others don't have to guess. Instead of snapping at a partner because you're secretly overwhelmed, you can say, *I feel anxious and need some reassurance.* Instead of withdrawing from a friend, you can say, *I feel hurt by what happened and need to talk about it.* This honesty builds trust and intimacy, because it allows others to meet the real you instead of a mask.

Perhaps most importantly, emotional awareness supports self-trust. Each time you accurately identify what you feel, you prove to yourself that your inner signals are valid. This directly counters the critic's message that your emotions are wrong or untrustworthy. As trust grows, you become less dependent on external approval to know how to act. You learn to check inward first, listening to your own body and heart as reliable guides.

Building emotional awareness is a gradual process. At first, you may only notice feelings after the fact. Then you'll start noticing them in the moment. Eventually, you'll anticipate them before they overwhelm you. This growth is not linear—some days will feel easy, others will feel confusing. But every moment of noticing counts. Each acknowledgment, no matter how small, strengthens the connection between your adult self and the inner child who longs to be heard.

In truth, emotional awareness is not just a skill—it is an act of reclamation. It is reclaiming the parts of yourself that were silenced, dismissed, or ignored. It is telling the inner child: *Your feelings matter. I want to hear them. I will not turn away.* And in that act of listening, you begin to live not only with more clarity but also with more freedom.

Why Emotions Matter

For a long time, emotions were dismissed as distractions—irrational impulses that got in the way of clear thinking. Many of us absorbed this belief early. We were told to calm down, toughen up, stop being so sensitive. Over time, we learned to mistrust feelings and rely only on logic. The problem with this approach is that emotions are not obstacles. They are information. They tell us what matters, where our limits are, and how experiences affect us. Ignoring them is like ignoring the fuel gauge in your car—you can keep driving, but eventually you'll run out of energy or break down without warning.

Emotions serve a purpose. Fear alerts us to danger. Sadness signals loss. Anger points to injustice. Joy tells us what brings life. Even anxiety, uncomfortable as it is, can point to areas where we crave safety or control. When we treat emotions as problems instead of signals, we miss the wisdom they carry. We also disconnect from our inner child, who has always communicated primarily through feelings.

Without emotional awareness, people often fall into unhealthy patterns. They overwork to avoid sadness, lash out instead of admitting fear, or numb themselves with distractions because they can't tolerate discomfort. These coping mechanisms may provide temporary relief, but they prevent real healing. The truth beneath the surface never goes away—it simply waits, demanding to be heard in stronger and stronger ways.

By contrast, paying attention to emotions creates freedom. When you can say, *I feel anxious right now,* you are no longer at the mercy of invisible forces. Naming the feeling brings it into the light, where it can be addressed. You can choose how to respond instead of reacting blindly. This shift is small but transformative.

Emotional awareness also deepens relationships. When you can express your feelings clearly, you invite others to connect more authentically. Instead of expecting people to guess, you give them the chance to respond to your truth. Saying, *I feel hurt,* may be uncomfortable, but it builds intimacy in ways that silence never can.

Most importantly, emotions connect you to yourself. They remind you that you are not a machine meant only to produce and perform. You are a whole person, with inner signals that deserve attention. Listening to those signals is an act of respect—for your body, your heart, and the child inside who has waited a long time to be heard.

Recognizing and Naming Feelings

Many adults can describe what they think in detail but freeze when asked what they feel. Instead of naming an emotion, they respond with, *I'm fine, I'm stressed,* or *I don't know.* This difficulty is not a flaw—it is the result of years of conditioning. If you grew up in an environment where feelings were dismissed or punished, ignoring them became a survival skill. But ignoring feelings doesn't erase them. They remain in the body, influencing choices, fueling anxiety, and shaping relationships. The first step in reclaiming this lost part of yourself is learning to recognize and name emotions with precision.

Moving Beyond "Good" and "Bad"

Most people describe emotions in broad strokes: good, bad, happy, sad. While this is a start, it misses the richness of emotional experience. Think of anger, for example. There is irritation, frustration, resentment, rage—each distinct, each carrying a different message. The same is true for sadness: disappointment, grief, loneliness, hopelessness. By broadening your emotional vocabulary, you become better able to understand what's really happening inside you.

Using a feelings list or wheel can help. These tools group emotions into categories, offering words you might not normally consider. When you pause to ask yourself not just, *Am I sad?* but, *Am I lonely? Am I grieving? Am I discouraged?* you sharpen awareness. Precision matters because different emotions call for different responses. Loneliness may call for connection, grief for space, discouragement for encouragement.

The Role of Attention

Recognition begins with paying attention. Emotions often arrive quietly, in the background of daily life. If you are distracted or constantly rushing, you may miss them until they grow overwhelming. Building awareness means slowing down enough to notice. Pause during the day and ask: *What am I feeling right now?* The answer might not come easily at first, but the act of asking signals to your mind and body that feelings are welcome.

Mindfulness practices can support this. Taking a few minutes to focus on your breath, noticing sensations without judgment, trains you to observe what arises internally. Over time, this practice makes it easier to catch emotions in the moment instead of only after they've spilled over into action.

Separating Thought from Feeling

Another challenge in naming emotions is distinguishing them from thoughts. A thought sounds like, *I'm failing at this job.* A feeling sounds like, *I feel anxious,* or *I feel ashamed.* The critic often disguises thoughts as facts, making them harder to recognize. But when you pause and strip away the story, you often find the emotion beneath it. *I'm failing* becomes, *I feel scared I'm not good enough.* Identifying the emotion under the thought shifts the focus from judgment to understanding.

The Power of Naming

Research shows that naming emotions reduces their intensity. This process, sometimes called "name it to tame it," works because language engages parts of the brain that calm the nervous system. Saying, *I feel angry* creates distance between you and the emotion. It doesn't erase it, but it makes it more manageable. Instead of being consumed by anger, you are a person noticing anger. That small separation creates room for choice.

Patterns and Triggers

Naming emotions also reveals patterns. You may notice that certain situations consistently trigger anxiety, or that certain relationships regularly bring up resentment. Recognizing these patterns gives you valuable information about where boundaries need to be strengthened or where healing is still unfinished. Triggers are not signs of weakness—they are invitations to pay attention. Each one points to an area where the inner child still seeks safety.

Practicing in Real Time

In daily life, practicing recognition means pausing in the middle of experiences, not just reflecting afterward. If you notice your shoulders tightening in a meeting, silently ask, *What am I feeling right now?* If you feel restless scrolling through your phone, ask, *What's underneath this? Am I bored, lonely, anxious?* The more often you practice, the quicker recognition becomes.

At first, it may feel awkward or even frustrating. You might mislabel feelings or feel uncertain. That's normal. Emotional awareness is a skill, and like any skill, it takes repetition. Each attempt, even if imperfect, strengthens your connection to yourself.

Why This Matters for Healing

Recognizing and naming feelings is not just an intellectual exercise. It is a way of validating your inner child. For years, that child may have been told, *Stop crying, Don't be angry,* or *You're too sensitive.* Every time you name a feeling now, you send a different message: *I hear you. Your emotions matter. I won't dismiss you anymore.* That simple act of acknowledgment begins to heal the old wounds of neglect.

Building this skill changes everything. Instead of being swept away by emotions or disconnected from them, you become an active participant in your inner life. You know when you are sad, when you are joyful, when you are afraid. You stop running on autopilot and start living with awareness. And in that awareness lies freedom—the freedom to respond, to choose, and to live authentically.

The Body as a Guide to Awareness

Many people think of emotions as something that happens only in the mind, but in reality, feelings live in the body. Long before we can name what we are experiencing, our bodies give us signals: a racing heart, tight shoulders, a sinking stomach, restless legs. These sensations are not random—they are the body's way of communicating emotion. Learning to listen to these signals is one of the most powerful ways to build emotional awareness.

Think of a time you felt anxious. Chances are, your body reacted before your mind fully understood what was happening. Maybe your chest felt tight, or your breath became shallow. By the time you thought, *I'm nervous,* your body had already sent the message. The same is true for anger, which often shows up as heat in the face, tension in the jaw, or clenched fists. Sadness may bring heaviness in the chest or tears in the eyes. Joy often feels like lightness, warmth, or ease. The body speaks first, and emotions follow.

The challenge is that many of us were trained to ignore these signals. As children, when we cried, we were told to stop. When we were afraid, we were told to toughen up. When we were angry, we were told to calm down. Over time, we learned to disconnect from the body's wisdom. We overrode signals of fatigue with caffeine, signals of hunger with busy schedules, signals of sadness with distraction. The more we ignored, the quieter those signals seemed—until they began to erupt in more dramatic ways, like chronic stress, illness, or emotional outbursts.

Reconnecting to the body begins with simple observation. Pause throughout the day and ask yourself: *What sensations am I noticing right now?* You might discover tension in your neck, butterflies in your stomach, or heaviness in your arms. Don't rush to judge or analyze—just notice. Over time, you'll begin to recognize patterns: tightness that signals anxiety, heaviness that signals sadness, restlessness that signals anger or frustration.

Breathwork can support this awareness. By slowing your breathing and paying attention to the rise and fall of your chest, you create space to notice sensations more clearly. Sometimes emotions feel overwhelming because they move too quickly to identify. Slowing the breath slows the experience, giving you time to recognize what's happening.

Movement is another powerful tool. Gentle practices like yoga, stretching, or walking can help you reconnect with physical sensations. As you move, pay attention to how different emotions show up in the body. You may notice that sadness makes you move more slowly, while joy brings a bounce to your step. These observations remind you that emotions are not just concepts—they are lived experiences in your body.

Journaling about body sensations can deepen the practice. Instead of writing, *I felt anxious today,* you might write, *My stomach was in knots before the meeting, and my chest felt heavy.* This specificity helps you draw connections between body signals and emotions. Over time, you'll become fluent in your body's language, able to catch feelings earlier and respond more effectively.

The body also offers a path to healing emotions that feel stuck. Sometimes feelings linger because they were never fully expressed. For example, if you were taught to suppress anger, the tension may remain in your body long after the triggering event. Practices like shaking, deep breathing, or even crying can release stored energy, allowing the emotion to move through instead of staying trapped.

Listening to the body is also a way of honoring the inner child. As children, our bodies felt emotions intensely—crying freely, laughing loudly, trembling when scared. When those natural expressions were silenced, the child learned to shut down. By paying attention to your body now, you tell that child: *I hear you. I won't ignore your signals anymore.* This act of listening is a profound form of self-respect.

The more you practice, the more you realize that the body is not your enemy. It is your ally, constantly sending messages about what you need. Sometimes the message is, *Rest.* Sometimes it is, *Speak up.* Sometimes it is, *You are safe now, it's okay to let go.* Emotional awareness becomes easier when you learn to trust those signals instead of overriding them.

In the end, the body is a compass for emotional truth. It grounds you in the present, cutting through the critic's noise and reminding you of what's real. By listening, you not only understand your emotions better—you reconnect with the part of you that has always known how to feel.

Integrating Emotional Awareness into Daily Life

Recognizing emotions in a quiet moment of reflection is one thing. Applying that awareness in the middle of everyday life is another. The stress of work, the demands of family, and the speed of daily routines can make it easy to slip back into old habits of ignoring or suppressing feelings. Integration is about making emotional awareness a natural part of how you live, not just something you practice occasionally.

The first step in integration is creating intentional pauses. Life rarely slows down on its own, so you have to build in moments to check in. These pauses don't need to be long. Taking thirty seconds before a meeting to ask, *How am I feeling right now?* can make a difference. Checking in while brushing your teeth, waiting at a red light, or pouring coffee turns ordinary moments into opportunities for self-connection.

Language is another tool for integration. Make it a habit to describe your emotions in words, even if only to yourself. Saying, *I feel nervous about this presentation* or *I feel lonely tonight* helps bring emotions into conscious awareness. When you practice naming feelings in small, everyday moments, you prepare yourself to do the same when the stakes are higher—during conflict, disappointment, or stress.

Relationships are where integration becomes most powerful. Emotional awareness allows you to communicate honestly instead of expecting others to guess what you need. Instead of withdrawing when upset, you might say, *I feel hurt and need some space.* Instead of snapping at a partner, you might admit, *I'm anxious right now, and I need reassurance.* These small acts of honesty build trust and reduce misunderstandings. They also remind your inner child that it is safe to express feelings openly.

Integration also means planning for difficult emotions before they arrive. Everyone experiences stress, anger, and sadness. By deciding ahead of time how you will respond, you give yourself a roadmap. For example, you might decide: *When I feel overwhelmed, I will step outside for fresh air instead of pushing through.* Or, *When I feel angry, I will write for ten minutes before responding.* These strategies prevent emotions from controlling your actions while still giving them space to be acknowledged.

Routine practices strengthen this integration. Journaling for five minutes each evening about what you felt that day helps solidify the habit of noticing. A weekly check-in, where you ask yourself, *What emotions showed up most this week?* can reveal patterns. Mindfulness or breathing exercises, practiced consistently, train your nervous system to stay open to emotions rather than shutting down. These routines turn awareness from a skill you practice into part of who you are.

Workplaces and social settings provide unique challenges, but awareness can be integrated here too. Before responding to an email that sparks frustration, take a breath and ask, *What am I feeling?* Before agreeing to another responsibility, ask, *Do I actually want to do this, or am I afraid of disappointing someone?* These questions may seem small, but over time, they protect your energy and help align your actions with your authentic self.

It's also helpful to create supportive environments. Surround yourself with people who welcome emotional honesty. Share your awareness with trusted friends: *I've been practicing noticing my feelings more, and today I realized I was anxious instead of angry.* Speaking these discoveries out loud reinforces them. Being around others who value emotions reduces the shame that can come with expressing them.

The critic may resist this process, warning you that being emotional makes you weak or dramatic. But integration proves otherwise. Each time you acknowledge and act on your emotions in daily life, you strengthen trust in yourself. You show your inner child that feelings are not dangerous—they are part of being human. That trust becomes the foundation for resilience.

In the end, integration is about weaving awareness into the rhythm of life. It's not about perfect tracking or constant introspection. It's about creating enough space in your daily routine to notice, name, and respond to emotions in real time. With practice, emotional awareness stops being something you do and becomes part of how you live.

When awareness is integrated, life feels more grounded. Decisions align more closely with your true needs. Relationships become clearer and more authentic. Stress no longer builds silently but is addressed before it overwhelms. Most importantly, the inner child within you feels seen and heard, not just in moments of reflection but in the flow of everyday life. That steady presence—of listening, acknowledging, and caring—is what transforms awareness into lasting healing.

Chapter 7:
Reconnecting with Joy and Play

For many adults, joy and play feel like distant memories. Childhood once held spontaneous laughter, make-believe games, and carefree moments where time seemed to disappear. But somewhere along the way, responsibility, stress, and the inner critic replaced that lightness. Many people don't even realize how much joy they've lost until they try to relax and feel restless, guilty, or empty. Reconnecting with joy and play is not about ignoring responsibilities—it is about reclaiming a vital part of your humanity that was buried under years of self-criticism and people-pleasing.

The inner child within you is the keeper of joy. Long before you learned to hide your feelings or shape yourself to meet others' expectations, that child knew how to delight in simple things: the feel of grass under bare feet, the rhythm of a favorite song, the thrill of chasing bubbles. These moments were not trivial. They were the building blocks of creativity, resilience, and emotional connection. When joy and play are cut off, life becomes survival instead of living.

One reason adults lose touch with joy is the belief that play is unproductive. In a culture that values achievement and efficiency, time spent laughing, exploring, or simply being can feel wasteful. The critic reinforces this message: *You should be doing something useful. You don't have time for fun.* But joy is not a distraction—it is fuel. Play refreshes the mind, heals the body, and opens space for creativity that problem-solving alone cannot provide.

Another reason joy feels distant is the association of play with childhood. Many adults carry shame about silliness or fun, fearing they'll be judged as immature. But play is not limited to children. Adults need it just as much, though it may take different forms:

hobbies, sports, creative expression, adventure, humor. The form doesn't matter as much as the spirit—engaging in something for no reason other than enjoyment.

Reconnecting with joy requires permission. Permission to rest without guilt. Permission to laugh without apology. Permission to spend time on activities that don't produce money, progress, or external approval. For many, this feels radical, even rebellious, because it contradicts years of conditioning. But the moment you give yourself permission, you create space for the inner child to come forward.

One way to begin is to remember what once brought you joy. Think back to childhood or adolescence. Did you love drawing, singing, riding bikes, climbing trees, telling stories? Often, those early joys leave clues about what still lights you up today. You may not climb trees anymore, but maybe hiking or gardening stirs the same aliveness. You may not play with dolls, but maybe creative writing or acting taps into that imaginative spark.

Joy also comes from curiosity. Children naturally explore without worrying about outcomes. As adults, we can practice the same mindset by trying new experiences without attaching judgment. Take a dance class, learn a new recipe, explore a hobby you've never considered. The goal is not to be good at it but to experience the pleasure of discovery.

Play is also deeply relational. Laughter with friends, games with family, shared adventures—these create bonds that logic and conversation alone cannot. Many relationships weaken because partners or friends stop playing together. Bringing back lightness through humor, games, or shared fun can revive connection. In these moments, the inner child in each person recognizes the other, building intimacy on a level deeper than words.

The critic will likely resist. It may whisper that you're wasting time, that you look foolish, or that you don't deserve joy. But each time you allow yourself to play, you weaken that voice. You prove that life is not only about productivity or perfection. You remind yourself that you are more than your achievements—you are a human being capable of delight.

Reconnecting with joy also heals the nervous system. Play reduces stress hormones, boosts energy, and strengthens resilience. It reminds your body what safety feels like, countering years of hypervigilance or pressure. In this way, joy is not a luxury but a necessity, especially for those healing from childhood wounds.

Integrating joy into daily life doesn't require huge changes. It can be as simple as pausing to watch a sunset, listening to music that makes you dance, or laughing at a silly video. Small doses of joy accumulate, gradually shifting your internal climate from tension to lightness. Over time, these moments retrain your system to expect not just survival but pleasure.

Ultimately, reconnecting with joy and play is about giving your inner child what was once lost: freedom. Freedom to explore, to laugh, to express without fear of judgment. Freedom to live not only for approval but for aliveness itself. By honoring joy, you don't regress to childhood—you integrate it into adulthood, creating a life that is both responsible and vibrant.

This chapter marks an important turn in healing. Up to now, much of the work has been about confronting pain—the critic, the wounds, the patterns of people-pleasing. Joy is the other side of healing. It is what makes the effort worthwhile. When you reclaim play, you remind yourself that healing is not just about less suffering—it is about more living.

The Role of Joy in Healing

When people think about healing, they often imagine hard work: therapy sessions, confronting painful memories, setting boundaries, practicing self-compassion. All of this is true and necessary. But healing is not only about easing pain—it is also about making room for joy. Joy is not a luxury that comes after the hard work is done; it is part of the work itself. It nourishes the nervous system, balances the weight of grief, and reminds you that life can hold beauty as well as struggle.

Joy heals because it restores balance. Trauma and criticism train the brain to scan constantly for danger. The inner child learns to expect disappointment, rejection, or punishment. Over time, this vigilance becomes the default state, making it hard to relax. Joy interrupts that cycle. Even brief moments of laughter or play tell your body: *It is safe to let go.* These signals calm stress responses, release tension, and open space for creativity and connection.

Another reason joy is essential is that it reconnects you to your authentic self. Many people-pleasers spend so much time shaping themselves for others that they lose touch with what actually feels good. Joy acts as a compass, pointing you back toward your true desires. When you feel lightness in your body, when time seems to disappear because you are absorbed in something fun, you are touching the self beneath the critic and the roles. These moments remind you of who you were before fear took over.

Joy also builds resilience. It's easy to believe that resilience comes only from toughness, but research shows the opposite. People who laugh, who find small pleasures, who allow themselves play, recover from setbacks more quickly. Joy gives you the energy to keep going when challenges arise. It creates space between struggles, so life does not feel like an endless string of battles.

The inner child, especially, needs joy to feel safe. When healing focuses only on pain, the child inside may feel trapped in old wounds. Offering joy—through play, creativity, or simple delight—signals that the story does not end with suffering. There is room for laughter too. In this way, joy becomes not just a byproduct of healing but an active ingredient in it.

Healing is not complete when pain is reduced. It is complete when you also feel alive, free, and capable of delight. That is why joy matters: it restores wholeness. It reminds you that your story includes not only wounds but also the possibility of light.

Rediscovering Childhood Sources of Play

When you think back to childhood, certain memories may stand out— not necessarily grand events, but small moments when joy felt natural and effortless. Riding a bike until the streetlights came on. Drawing pictures with crayons. Making up stories with friends. Singing loudly without worrying who was listening. These activities were not planned for productivity or achievement. They were pure expressions of curiosity, energy, and imagination. For many adults, those activities have long been abandoned, pushed aside by responsibility and the critic's demands. Yet they still hold the key to reconnecting with joy today.

The inner child often remembers what the adult forgets. What you loved as a child usually reflects something deeply true about your spirit. Maybe you were drawn to nature, spending hours collecting rocks or climbing trees. Maybe you loved music, inventing songs or dancing around your room. Maybe you enjoyed building things, from sandcastles to forts. These early joys may look different in adulthood, but the essence remains the same. The child who loved nature may find joy in hiking or gardening. The one who loved music may reconnect through concerts or karaoke. The builder may discover satisfaction in cooking, woodworking, or design. The details change, but the thread of joy runs continuously.

A helpful practice is to make a list of activities you loved before the world told you to be serious. Write down as many as you can remember, no matter how silly they seem. Did you love pretending to be a superhero? Dressing up? Playing board games? These memories often bring a smile even before you try them again. Then, choose one to reintroduce into your life in some form. Start small. If you loved drawing, buy a sketchbook and doodle for ten minutes. If you loved being outside, commit to a short walk each day. If you loved games, invite a friend to play cards or a video game. The goal is not to recreate childhood exactly, but to bring back the spirit of play.

At first, this can feel awkward. The critic may jump in quickly: *This is childish. You look ridiculous. You're wasting time.* But notice how those thoughts echo the voices that once silenced your play as a child. Choosing to play anyway is an act of rebellion against those old rules. It is saying to your inner child: *Your joy matters, and I will not take it away again.*

Another way to rediscover childhood joy is through sensory experiences. Children naturally delight in sights, sounds, textures, and tastes. Running barefoot on grass, blowing bubbles, spinning in circles, eating ice cream on a hot day—these simple sensations brought deep satisfaction. As adults, we often rush past them. But slowing down to notice sensory pleasures can reignite that spark. Try lying on the grass and watching clouds, listening to a favorite song at full volume, or savoring a favorite treat without distraction. These small acts remind your body what play feels like.

Imagination is another forgotten doorway to play. Children invent entire worlds with cardboard boxes and stuffed animals. Adults may feel silly doing the same, but imagination still has power. Storytelling, acting, role-playing games, or creative writing all tap into the same ability to dream beyond the ordinary. Even daydreaming—allowing your mind to wander without purpose—can bring moments of freedom and delight.

Sharing childhood joys with others makes them even richer. Invite friends or family to join in activities you once loved. Have a picnic, play a board game, or dance in the living room. Children rarely play alone for long; they seek connection through shared fun. Reintroducing this spirit into adult relationships strengthens bonds and makes joy more sustainable.

It's also important to release comparison. Children don't stop drawing because they aren't "artists," or stop singing because they aren't "good enough." They play for the sake of play. As adults, perfectionism often kills joy before it begins. To rediscover play, you must let go of the need to be good at it. The goal is not skill—it is delight. A crooked drawing, an off-key song, a clumsy dance can all be sources of joy if you approach them with openness.

Rediscovering childhood sources of play is not about regressing to immaturity. It is about reclaiming the parts of you that were once silenced. It is telling yourself that joy does not need justification, that laughter does not require permission. These activities may seem small, but they carry profound healing. They reconnect you to the child who once lived freely and remind you that even as an adult, that spirit still lives inside you.

Creating Space for Joy in Adult Life

Reconnecting with joy as an adult is not just about remembering what once made you happy—it's about deliberately making room for it now. Modern life is often crowded with responsibilities: work, family, bills, endless to-do lists. Joy tends to be pushed to the margins, treated as optional or even indulgent. But if joy is essential to healing, it cannot be something you fit in only when everything else is finished. It must be given space, the same way you give space to sleep, food, and other necessities.

The first step is to redefine joy as a priority, not an afterthought. This shift requires challenging old beliefs. The critic may insist, *Fun is for children. You don't have time for that. You should be working.* But joy is not a distraction from life—it's part of what makes life worth living. Without it, responsibility becomes drudgery. With it, even the hardest work feels more balanced. By treating joy as important, you send a message to yourself and your inner child: *Your happiness matters as much as your productivity.*

Creating space for joy often begins with small adjustments. You don't need to overhaul your entire life. Start by identifying small windows of time where joy can fit naturally. Ten minutes in the morning to listen to music, half an hour on the weekend to draw, a walk during lunch to feel the sun. These micro-moments may seem insignificant, but they accumulate, reminding your body and mind what lightness feels like.

Boundaries play a key role here. If your schedule is packed with obligations, you may need to say no to something else in order to say yes to joy. This can feel uncomfortable at first, especially if you're used to prioritizing everyone else's needs. But every time you choose joy over obligation, you strengthen self-trust. You prove that your life is not only about serving others—it's also about honoring your own aliveness.

Another way to create space is through rituals. Rituals anchor joy into daily life, making it less likely to be forgotten. For example, you might create a Friday night tradition of cooking a fun meal, a Sunday morning ritual of reading a novel with coffee, or a weekly outing with a friend who makes you laugh. These predictable patterns create anticipation and structure, reminding you that joy is a regular part of life, not an accident.

It's also helpful to notice where joy already exists and expand it. Maybe you smile when you hear a certain song—play it more often. Maybe you enjoy time in nature—schedule regular walks or hikes. Maybe you feel light when you're creative—dedicate a space in your home for art or writing. Joy does not always need to be invented from scratch. Often, it's about noticing what already sparks delight and allowing yourself more of it.

Social support makes joy easier to sustain. Share your intention with people who value fun and play. Join communities centered on hobbies, sports, or creative expression. Surrounding yourself with others who embrace joy helps counteract the critic's voice and reduces the guilt of prioritizing it. In those spaces, laughter and play are normalized, reminding you that joy is not frivolous but human.

Finally, creating space for joy requires patience. If you've been disconnected from fun for a long time, joy may feel distant or awkward at first. That doesn't mean it's gone—it means it needs time to resurface. Approach it gently, without pressure. Allow yourself to try different activities, to experiment, to rediscover what feels alive. Trust that joy will return, not as a forced obligation but as a natural response once space is made for it.

In adulthood, joy doesn't erase responsibilities, but it gives them balance. It reminds you that life is not just about enduring but about living. By creating space for joy, you heal the child within who once laughed freely, and you give yourself permission to live with both responsibility and delight.

The Power of Play in Relationships

Play is often seen as an individual activity—something you do to relax, explore, or entertain yourself. But one of its greatest powers is the way it strengthens relationships. Shared laughter, games, and moments of silliness create bonds that no amount of serious conversation can replicate. When people play together, they lower defenses, drop roles, and meet each other with openness. For those healing from childhood wounds, bringing play into relationships is a way of reclaiming connection without fear.

Think about how children form friendships. They don't ask for résumés or checklists. They run to the playground, suggest a game, and within minutes they're laughing together. That natural ease may seem lost in adulthood, but it can be revived. Play is the bridge. It bypasses the critic's voice, which is quick to judge or compare, and instead invites spontaneity.

In romantic relationships, play keeps connection alive. Over time, many couples slip into routines centered on logistics: work schedules, chores, finances. While these responsibilities are necessary, they can drain energy if they become the only focus. Injecting play—through jokes, games, adventures, or simple silliness—brings lightness back into the bond. It reminds partners why they chose each other in the first place, not only as co-managers of life but as companions in joy.

Friendships, too, thrive on play. Shared hobbies, sports, inside jokes, or creative projects create a sense of belonging that words alone cannot. Laughter builds trust. When you can be silly with someone, you know you are safe. Play tells the nervous system: *This relationship is not only functional—it is nourishing.*

Families benefit as well. Parents who play with their children show them that connection is not only about discipline or structure but also about fun. Siblings who share games and humor create memories that last into adulthood. Even adult families can use play to heal old wounds, whether through shared activities, humor, or traditions that bring everyone together in lighthearted ways.

The critic often resists play in relationships, whispering, *You'll look foolish. You're being immature. People won't take you seriously.* But the truth is that play deepens trust rather than weakening it. When you allow yourself to laugh or be silly with someone, you show vulnerability in a safe way. You let them see a side of you unguarded by performance. Far from undermining respect, this kind of vulnerability often makes respect grow stronger.

Practical ways to invite play into relationships are simple. Start with humor—share funny stories, watch comedies together, or let yourself laugh freely at silly moments. Play games, whether board games, sports, or even small challenges like cooking competitions. Explore adventures, from trying new foods to traveling to unfamiliar places. Even inside routines, play can be woven in—singing while cleaning, making up stories during a walk, or turning chores into small competitions.

It's important to note that play looks different for everyone. What feels fun for one person may feel stressful for another. The key is to experiment and communicate. Ask, *What's something playful we could try together?* This question itself often sparks ideas and shows willingness to connect in lighthearted ways.

For those healing from people-pleasing, play in relationships has an extra layer of meaning. It allows you to connect without performance. Instead of giving only to please, you participate in joy for its own sake. This balance strengthens bonds because both people share in the fun, rather than one constantly sacrificing.

The power of play in relationships is not about ignoring serious matters. Life will always include challenges, and honest conversations are essential. But without play, relationships become heavy. With it, even difficulties feel more manageable, because laughter provides resilience. A relationship that can hold both tears and laughter is one that can endure.

In the end, play is more than entertainment—it is a form of intimacy. It creates shared memories, lightens burdens, and reminds us that connection is meant to bring joy as well as support. When you allow play into your relationships, you heal not only yourself but also the spaces between you and the people you love.

Chapter 8:
Cultivating Self-Trust

One of the deepest wounds left by childhood criticism, neglect, or people-pleasing is the erosion of self-trust. When you grow up in an environment where your feelings were dismissed, your boundaries ignored, or your needs minimized, you learn to doubt your own signals. Instead of asking, *What do I want?* or *What feels right to me?* you ask, *What do they expect? What will keep me safe?* Over time, you lose confidence in your own inner compass.

Cultivating self-trust means reclaiming that compass. It means relearning how to rely on your own judgment, honoring your emotions, and believing that you can handle challenges without abandoning yourself. Self-trust does not mean you will never make mistakes. It means you trust yourself to respond with honesty, compassion, and resilience when mistakes happen.

The absence of self-trust often shows up in subtle ways. You second-guess every decision, from what to order at a restaurant to whether to take a new job. You seek reassurance constantly, needing others to tell you that you're okay. You feel paralyzed in conflict, afraid that choosing your truth will cost you love or belonging. These patterns are not signs of weakness—they are the residue of environments that taught you to outsource your sense of worth.

Rebuilding trust begins with small, intentional choices. Each time you ask yourself, *What do I truly want right now?* and honor the answer, you send a message to your inner child: *Your voice matters. I am listening.* At first, this may be as simple as choosing rest when you're tired or declining an invitation when you need quiet. These acts may feel insignificant, but they are the foundation of trust. Over time, they accumulate into a steady belief that you can rely on yourself.

Listening to your body is part of this process. Your body is often the first to signal whether something feels safe or not. A knot in your stomach, a sense of heaviness, or a burst of energy—these sensations are guides. Self-trust means noticing them, respecting them, and taking them seriously instead of dismissing them as inconvenient. When you act in alignment with your body's signals, you strengthen the bond between your adult self and your inner child.

Another element of self-trust is learning to tolerate mistakes. The critic insists that one wrong step proves you are incompetent or unworthy. But mistakes are not evidence against you—they are evidence that you are human. Each time you treat a mistake with compassion, you teach yourself that failure is survivable. This makes risk-taking possible again. Without this tolerance, you remain frozen, too afraid to move forward. With it, you grow braver, knowing that even if things don't go as planned, you will not abandon yourself.

Boundaries also play a role. Self-trust grows when you act consistently with your values, even when others disagree. Each time you say no when you mean no, or yes when you mean yes, you prove to yourself that your word is reliable. Over time, this reliability becomes a source of pride. You no longer feel pulled in every direction by external demands, because you know your choices reflect who you are.

Of course, rebuilding self-trust is not always straightforward. Years of self-doubt do not vanish overnight. At first, you may still question yourself, still look outward for reassurance. That's okay. The practice is not about perfection but persistence. Every small act of honoring your truth, no matter how shaky, strengthens the foundation.

Relationships often test self-trust. When you speak up for your needs, you may fear rejection. When you set boundaries, you may worry about angering others. But each time you choose authenticity, you reinforce the belief that you can survive discomfort. Trust in yourself grows not by avoiding conflict but by proving that you can stay true to yourself within it.

Journaling can support this practice. Write about moments when you listened to your inner signals and how it felt. Record small victories, like honoring your fatigue or expressing an unpopular opinion. Looking back at these records reminds you of your growth and provides evidence against the critic's voice.

Self-trust also means learning to rely less on external validation. Praise feels good, but when it becomes the only measure of worth, you remain dependent on others' approval. Cultivating self-trust shifts the focus inward. Instead of asking, *Do they approve of me?* you ask, *Do I approve of how I showed up?* This doesn't mean ignoring feedback, but it does mean making your own sense of integrity the final authority.

At its core, cultivating self-trust is an act of reparenting. It is becoming the reliable caregiver your younger self needed—the one who listens, protects, and believes in you. Each act of self-honoring is like telling your inner child: *I won't betray you. You can count on me now.* Over time, this relationship becomes steady enough that you no longer live in fear of abandonment. You know you have yourself.

Self-trust does not erase uncertainty or guarantee perfect choices. What it offers is steadiness. With self-trust, you can face uncertainty without crumbling, because you know you won't turn against yourself. You can risk, explore, and grow, because you have a foundation strong enough to hold you.

In the journey of healing the inner child, self-trust is the turning point. It is the moment when you stop outsourcing your worth and begin living from within. Pain may still exist, challenges may still arise, but you face them differently—not as someone desperate for approval, but as someone grounded in their own truth. And that shift changes everything.

Why Self-Trust Is Hard to Build

Many people assume self-trust should come naturally. After all, who else could you rely on more than yourself? But for those who grew up in environments where their needs were ignored, their feelings dismissed, or their choices punished, self-trust is one of the hardest things to cultivate. Instead of learning to listen inward, they learned to look outward—for approval, guidance, or safety. By the time adulthood arrives, the inner compass feels broken.

The root of this difficulty lies in childhood experiences. If you expressed sadness and were told to "stop crying," you learned that your feelings couldn't be trusted. If you said no and were ignored, you learned that your boundaries didn't matter. If you made a choice and were punished, you learned that your judgment was flawed. Slowly, you internalized the belief that your inner signals were unreliable or even dangerous. To survive, you silenced them and replaced them with strategies designed to keep others happy.

This survival strategy works for a while—it may even earn praise for being agreeable, responsible, or selfless. But underneath, it creates a fracture. You move through life disconnected from your own wants and needs. Decisions feel paralyzing because you don't know what's truly yours and what's been shaped by others' expectations. The critic deepens this fracture, constantly second-guessing every impulse and demanding reassurance before you act.

Cultural messages make the problem worse. Many societies prize conformity, productivity, and external success. Children are often praised for following rules more than for following their curiosity. By adulthood, the idea of trusting your inner world can feel reckless, even selfish. No wonder so many people find themselves stuck in doubt, afraid to act without external validation.

It's important to understand that difficulty with self-trust is not a personal flaw. It is the predictable result of environments that discouraged authenticity. If you doubt yourself, it does not mean you are weak. It means you learned to survive by outsourcing your decisions. That skill may have kept you safe then, but it keeps you stuck now.

The good news is that self-trust can be rebuilt. Like any relationship, it grows through consistency and care. Each time you listen to your body, honor your emotions, or act in alignment with your values, you strengthen the bond with yourself. It may feel shaky at first, but with patience, that bond becomes steady.

Listening to Your Inner Signals

Rebuilding self-trust begins with learning to hear and respect the signals your body and emotions send you. These signals are not random—they are your internal guidance system, pointing you toward what feels safe, authentic, or aligned, and warning you when something feels off. The challenge is that many people have been conditioned to ignore or override these signals for so long that they barely notice them.

Think about how often you've pushed past fatigue to finish work, ignored hunger because you were too busy, or silenced anger because it felt dangerous to express. Over time, these choices send a message to your inner child: *Your signals don't matter.* Slowly, the connection weakens. Listening to your inner signals is about reversing that message and proving, day by day, that you are paying attention again.

The Body Speaks First

Before the mind forms words, the body responds. A knot in the stomach, tightness in the chest, or sudden heaviness often arrives before you consciously realize what you're feeling. These physical cues are important because they cut through the critic's noise. While the critic may argue that you're overreacting, your body's signals are harder to deny. A stomach in knots doesn't lie.

Begin by practicing body check-ins. A few times each day, pause and ask: *What sensations am I noticing right now?* Maybe your shoulders are tense, your hands restless, or your breathing shallow. Don't rush to fix anything—just notice. Over time, you'll begin to see connections: tension when you're anxious, lightness when you're excited, heaviness when you're sad. These observations rebuild the bridge between body and mind.

Emotional Cues as Guides

Emotions also serve as signals, but many people dismiss them as irrational or inconvenient. In reality, emotions provide crucial information. Anger may signal a boundary crossed. Sadness may signal loss or unmet need. Anxiety may signal a lack of safety. Joy may signal alignment. Listening doesn't mean obeying every emotion blindly; it means considering what the emotion is trying to communicate.

One useful practice is to pause when a strong emotion arises and ask: *What message is this emotion sending me?* For example, anger may be saying, *Pay attention—something here feels unfair.* Sadness may be saying, *Something important is missing.* By treating emotions as messengers rather than enemies, you begin to rebuild trust in their wisdom.

Learning to Distinguish Signals

At first, signals may feel confusing or contradictory. You may feel excitement and fear at the same time, or anger layered over sadness. That's normal—emotions are rarely simple. Part of listening is learning to sort through the layers. For example, beneath anger, you may discover hurt. Beneath anxiety, you may find the desire for reassurance. The more you practice curiosity, the clearer the signals become.

Journaling can help here. Writing about what you feel and where you feel it in your body often brings clarity. Over time, you may notice patterns: you feel drained after certain interactions, energized after others, anxious in specific situations. These patterns reveal which environments support your well-being and which undermine it.

Acting on Signals

Listening is only half of the equation. Self-trust grows when you act on what you hear. If your body says, *I need rest,* and you rest, trust strengthens. If your emotions say, *This doesn't feel safe,* and you set a boundary, trust deepens. Each time you respond, you prove to your inner child that you are reliable.

This doesn't mean you'll always act perfectly. Sometimes you'll override signals out of habit, fear, or circumstance. That's okay. What matters is returning to awareness, acknowledging what happened, and recommitting to listening. The goal is progress, not perfection.

Facing the Critic's Interference

The critic often tries to interfere with this process. When you notice fatigue, it may say, *Don't be lazy.* When you feel sadness, it may say, *Stop being dramatic.* When you want to say no, it may say, *You'll disappoint everyone.* Part of listening to your signals is recognizing when the critic tries to override them. In those moments, compassion becomes your ally. You can respond, *I hear the critic, but I choose to trust myself this time.*

Building Consistency

Like any relationship, trust is built through consistency. Listening once is helpful, but listening again and again creates reliability. Start with small commitments—drinking water when thirsty, resting when tired, speaking up when something feels off. Each small act sends the message: *I take my signals seriously.* Over time, this consistency transforms doubt into confidence.

Learning from Mistakes Without Shame

One of the greatest barriers to self-trust is the way we treat ourselves after making mistakes. For many people, errors are not just events—they are evidence of failure, proof that they are incompetent, careless, or unworthy. This reaction usually traces back to childhood. If mistakes were met with harsh punishment, ridicule, or withdrawal of affection, the inner child learned to associate error with danger. By adulthood, even small missteps can trigger a storm of shame.

The problem with shame is that it paralyzes growth. When you believe mistakes define you, you avoid risks, play it safe, and hesitate to try new things. The critic reinforces this fear, saying, *If you fail, you'll never recover. Don't even try.* Ironically, this avoidance creates more frustration, because life without risk is life without progress. Self-trust requires a different relationship to mistakes—one built on compassion and curiosity instead of shame.

Reframing Mistakes

The first step is to reframe what mistakes mean. Instead of treating them as proof of inadequacy, see them as information. A mistake simply shows you that a strategy didn't work, that more learning is needed, or that circumstances were not as expected. In this light, mistakes are not evidence against you—they are teachers. This perspective doesn't erase disappointment, but it removes the judgment that makes disappointment unbearable.

Responding with Compassion

When you make a mistake, notice the critic's response. Maybe it says, *You always mess things up*, or, *This is why no one trusts you.* Instead of joining in the attack, pause and respond with compassion. You might say to yourself, *I made an error, but I'm still worthy. I can learn from this.* Placing a hand on your heart or taking a slow breath can reinforce the message physically, calming the nervous system so shame doesn't take over.

Small Steps in Practice

Begin practicing with small mistakes. If you forget an appointment, resist the urge to spiral into self-condemnation. Instead, acknowledge what happened, apologize if necessary, and adjust your system for reminders. If you burn dinner, laugh if you can, and remember that imperfection is part of being human. Each small act of kindness toward yourself creates a foundation for handling bigger mistakes with grace.

Mistakes and Growth

Think about how children learn. They fall hundreds of times before walking. They mispronounce words before speaking fluently. No one sees these mistakes as failures—they are understood as part of learning. The same is true in adulthood. Every new skill, every new boundary, every new act of courage will include errors. Instead of seeing them as proof you can't change, recognize them as proof you are in the process of changing.

Separating Identity from Behavior

A crucial part of learning from mistakes is separating what you did from who you are. Behavior is changeable; identity is not up for debate. Saying, *I made a mistake,* keeps the focus on the action. Saying, *I am a failure,* turns the mistake into identity. Self-trust grows when you stop collapsing the two. You are not the sum of your errors. You are a human being learning in real time.

The Role of Repair

When mistakes affect others, self-trust also grows through repair. Apologizing sincerely, making amends, and taking responsibility strengthen your sense of integrity. The critic may fear that admitting mistakes will make you look weak, but the opposite is true. Repair builds trust with others and with yourself, because you prove you can face errors honestly without collapsing into shame.

Building Resilience

Over time, this new relationship with mistakes builds resilience. You no longer freeze at the possibility of failure, because you know you can recover. You stop outsourcing decisions, because even if things go wrong, you trust yourself to respond with honesty and care. This resilience is what allows growth to continue.

Mistakes are inevitable. What matters is not avoiding them but learning how to meet them. Each time you replace shame with compassion, you strengthen the bond with your inner child. You show them that mistakes are survivable, that love is not withdrawn when things go wrong, and that they can trust you to stay steady. That steady presence—calm, kind, and reliable—is the heart of self-trust.

Living Authentically Through Self-Trust

When you begin to rebuild self-trust, the changes in your daily life become unmistakable. Decisions feel lighter. Boundaries feel clearer. Relationships feel more balanced. But the most powerful shift is the sense of authenticity that emerges. Living authentically means showing up as who you are, not as who others expect you to be. And authenticity is impossible without self-trust.

For years, many people-pleasers have lived behind masks—smiling when they wanted to cry, agreeing when they wanted to refuse, performing competence when they felt uncertain. These masks were not chosen lightly. They were survival tools, built to avoid rejection or punishment. But over time, the masks become prisons. You begin to forget what your own face looks like beneath them. Cultivating self-trust is how you take the mask off.

Authenticity begins in small choices. It might look like ordering the food you actually want instead of what you think looks "healthier." It might look like admitting, *I don't know,* when you feel uncertain, instead of pretending to have the answer. It might look like telling a friend, *I need rest tonight,* instead of pushing yourself past exhaustion. Each small act proves to your inner child that it is safe to be real.

Self-trust also transforms relationships. When you no longer betray yourself to gain approval, connections become more genuine. Some relationships may fade, especially those built on your compliance, but the ones that remain grow stronger. People who value you for who you truly are will stay. Those who only valued what you gave them may resist. While this can be painful, it is also clarifying. Authenticity filters out relationships that cannot hold your truth.

Living authentically also brings clarity in decision-making. Instead of weighing every choice against others' expectations, you begin to ask, *Does this align with my values? Does this feel true to me?* At first, answering these questions may feel unfamiliar, but with practice, it becomes second nature. The result is a life that reflects your inner world rather than external demands.

The critic will resist this process. It may warn you that authenticity is risky—that people won't like you, that you'll fail, that you'll regret being honest. But each time you live authentically and survive the outcome, you weaken the critic's hold. You prove that authenticity may bring discomfort, but it also brings freedom.

Authenticity also means embracing imperfection. When you trust yourself, you no longer need to appear flawless to earn respect. You can admit mistakes, show vulnerability, and let others see your humanity. This openness often inspires respect rather than diminishing it, because people sense when they are in the presence of someone real.

Daily practices help anchor authenticity. Journaling about your values and checking if your actions align with them keeps you honest with yourself. Pausing before commitments and asking, *Am I saying yes because I want to, or because I'm afraid of rejection?* helps prevent old patterns from creeping in. Celebrating small moments of honesty—like expressing a genuine opinion or declining politely—reinforces the habit of living true.

Over time, living authentically through self-trust brings a sense of steadiness. You no longer feel pulled in every direction by others' desires. You stop doubting every choice. You know that even when things are hard, you will not abandon yourself. This steadiness doesn't eliminate pain or conflict, but it makes them easier to face. With authenticity, you know that whatever happens, you are aligned with yourself—and that alignment is priceless.

Ultimately, living authentically through self-trust is an act of liberation. It frees you from the critic's grip, from the endless chase for approval, from the exhaustion of masks. It allows you to meet the world as you truly are: imperfect, human, and whole. And in that honesty, you discover a life not only more peaceful but also more joyful, because it finally belongs to you.

Chapter 9:
Healing Through Relationships

Healing the inner child is deeply personal, but it is not something that happens in isolation. Relationships play a central role in how wounds are created, and they also hold the potential for repair. The ways we were treated in childhood—whether ignored, criticized, or pressured—shaped how we see ourselves. But the way we are treated in adulthood can reshape that view. When we experience respect, kindness, and genuine care from others, our nervous system begins to learn that connection can be safe.

Relationships act as mirrors. They reflect back the beliefs we carry about ourselves. If you secretly believe you are unworthy, you may unconsciously seek relationships that reinforce that belief—partners who dismiss you, friends who take without giving, workplaces that exploit your effort. These patterns are not random. They are familiar. They echo the dynamics you learned early on. Recognizing this is not about blame—it's about awareness. When you see the pattern, you gain the power to choose differently.

Healing through relationships begins with awareness of these old dynamics. Ask yourself: *Do I feel seen in my relationships? Do I feel free to be myself? Or do I shrink, perform, or silence parts of me to stay accepted?* Honest answers to these questions reveal where old wounds are still active. Sometimes, even relationships that look "fine" on the surface keep you stuck if they require constant self-betrayal.

Healthy relationships, by contrast, create space for authenticity. They allow you to say no without punishment, to express feelings without ridicule, to rest without guilt. These relationships do not demand perfection; they welcome imperfection as part of being human. For someone who grew up with criticism or neglect, this kind of acceptance can feel almost unbelievable at first. But slowly, consistent kindness begins to rebuild trust. The inner child learns: *This time, it's different. This time, I am safe.*

Of course, healing relationships are not only about receiving—they also require giving. When you practice compassion toward others, listen deeply, and respect their boundaries, you reinforce the same values you are learning to apply to yourself. In this way, relationships become laboratories for growth. Each interaction is a chance to practice authenticity, compassion, and respect.

Boundaries remain crucial here. Without them, relationships can easily slide into old patterns of self-sacrifice. Healing does not mean tolerating disrespect in the hope of repair. It means recognizing which relationships are capable of growth and which are not. Some connections will strengthen as you grow; others may fade. Letting go of relationships that cannot honor your truth is painful, but it also clears space for connections that nourish instead of drain.

One of the most powerful aspects of healing through relationships is co-regulation. Human nervous systems are wired to respond to each other. When someone offers calm presence, empathy, or gentle words, your body begins to settle too. This is why a hug can ease anxiety or a kind word can dissolve tension. For people whose childhoods lacked this soothing presence, receiving it in adulthood can be profoundly healing. It teaches the body what safety feels like.

Romantic relationships often bring these dynamics into sharp focus. Partners tend to trigger old wounds—abandonment fears, fear of rejection, fear of being "too much." While this can be painful, it also offers opportunity. Each trigger is a chance to practice new responses, to notice the critic's voice, and to communicate openly instead of shutting down. With a partner who values growth, these moments can deepen intimacy and rewrite old stories.

Friendships and chosen families also hold immense healing potential. Unlike childhood families, which we could not choose, adult friendships are built on mutual choice. Surrounding yourself with people who support your authenticity, who celebrate your joy, and who respect your boundaries is one of the greatest gifts you can give your inner child. In these relationships, you experience belonging without performance—a powerful antidote to people-pleasing.

Therapeutic relationships play a role too. A therapist, coach, or mentor who listens without judgment models the kind of care you may have missed as a child. Over time, their consistent presence helps you internalize a new voice—one of compassion instead of criticism. This voice then becomes part of your own self-talk, shaping how you relate to yourself even outside of the therapeutic space.

Healing through relationships does not mean relying on others to "fix" you. No one else can do the work of listening to your feelings, setting your boundaries, or choosing your truth. But relationships provide the context where your growth is tested, supported, and reinforced. They are the soil where new patterns take root.

The path is not always smooth. Some relationships will resist your growth. Some people will prefer the version of you who stayed silent and agreeable. As you change, they may push back. This is not a sign that you are wrong—it is a sign that you are breaking old patterns. Trust that the connections meant to support your authenticity will adapt, while those that cannot may need to fall away.

Ultimately, healing through relationships is about balance. You do not heal alone, and you do not heal by giving all of yourself away. You heal by allowing connection and protection to coexist. You allow others to see you, while also trusting yourself enough to walk away when a connection harms more than it helps. In this balance, you create a network of relationships that not only reflect your wounds but also nurture your wholeness.

Healing the inner child begins within, but it is completed in the presence of others. When you learn to show up authentically, receive care, and give care freely, you rewrite the script that once told you connection was dangerous. You discover that relationships can be places of safety, joy, and growth. And in those spaces, the child inside you finally feels at home.

Seeing Old Patterns in Relationships

The first step to healing through relationships is recognizing the patterns that repeat. Many people wonder why they keep ending up with partners who dismiss them, friends who take advantage, or workplaces that exploit their effort. On the surface, these patterns look like bad luck. In truth, they are echoes of early experiences.

As children, we learned how connection worked from the people closest to us. If love was conditional, we learned to perform to earn it. If boundaries were ignored, we learned to stay silent. If criticism was constant, we learned to expect rejection. These lessons became internalized as "normal," and as adults, we unconsciously gravitate toward what feels familiar—even if it hurts.

For example, someone who grew up with emotionally unavailable parents may find themselves drawn to distant partners. The lack of attention feels strangely comfortable, even if it leaves them unsatisfied. Someone who grew up being praised only for achievement may find themselves in friendships or jobs where their value depends on constant performance. These dynamics are not chosen consciously, but they reflect the old scripts still running beneath the surface.

Recognizing patterns requires honest reflection. Ask yourself:

- Do I feel like I can be my full self in this relationship?
- Do I often feel drained or anxious after interactions?
- Do I minimize my needs to keep the peace?

If the answers reveal discomfort, it doesn't mean you've failed. It means you're seeing clearly. Awareness is the first step toward change.

It's important to approach this awareness with compassion, not judgment. Falling into familiar patterns is not a sign of weakness—it is a sign that your nervous system is doing what it learned to do to survive. Once you see the pattern, you can begin to choose differently.

Breaking old patterns takes time. The critic may resist, warning you that new dynamics are unsafe or that you'll end up alone if you change. But each time you recognize a familiar script and pause before acting it out, you weaken its hold. You open the possibility of building relationships that don't repeat the past but create something new.

What Safe and Supportive Relationships Look Like

For someone who grew up with criticism, neglect, or inconsistency, safe and supportive relationships can feel almost foreign. You may know what unhealthy dynamics look like—they are familiar, even predictable—but struggle to imagine what healthy connection should feel like. Learning to identify the qualities of supportive relationships is essential, because it gives you a new template. Instead of repeating the past, you can begin to recognize and choose what truly nurtures you.

Emotional Safety

At the heart of a supportive relationship is emotional safety. This doesn't mean there are never disagreements, but it does mean you can express yourself without fear of ridicule, punishment, or abandonment. In safe relationships, you can say, *I feel hurt,* or *I need space,* and know the other person will listen rather than attack. Your emotions are taken seriously, even if the other person doesn't fully understand them. Over time, this consistency teaches your inner child that it is safe to be seen and heard.

Respect for Boundaries

Another marker of supportive relationships is respect for boundaries. In unhealthy dynamics, no often isn't accepted, and your limits are pushed until you give in. In supportive relationships, no is respected. You don't have to justify or apologize endlessly. Whether it's time, space, or emotional limits, the other person honors your boundary as a valid part of connection. This respect builds trust, showing you that closeness doesn't require sacrifice.

Reciprocity

Safe relationships are reciprocal. This doesn't mean everything is split evenly at all times, but there is a sense of balance. Both people give and both people receive. If you listen deeply when your friend is struggling, you can expect the same care when you're in need. If you compromise sometimes, your partner does too. This balance prevents the exhaustion and resentment that come from one-sided connections.

Consistency Over Perfection

Supportive relationships are consistent. You can rely on the other person to show up in ways that feel steady. They don't disappear when things get hard or swing between extremes of affection and withdrawal. Consistency doesn't mean perfection—everyone makes mistakes—but it does mean reliability. Apologies and repair happen when harm occurs, and the relationship doesn't collapse under pressure.

Encouragement and Growth

A safe relationship encourages your growth rather than resenting it. Unhealthy dynamics often keep you small, because your growth threatens the other person's control. Supportive relationships, by contrast, celebrate your progress. They may challenge you, but not from a place of tearing down—from a place of wanting to see you thrive. Being with people who genuinely root for you helps counter the critic's voice that insists you can't change.

Freedom to Be Imperfect

Perhaps one of the most healing qualities of supportive relationships is the freedom to be imperfect. In these connections, you don't have to perform or hide your flaws. You can admit when you're tired, when you've made a mistake, or when you're struggling. Instead of rejection, you're met with empathy or patience. For someone who grew up believing love had to be earned through performance, this freedom can feel revolutionary.

How It Feels in the Body

Sometimes the easiest way to recognize a safe relationship is through how your body feels. Do you feel tense and on guard, waiting for criticism? Or do you feel relaxed, able to breathe fully, maybe even lighter after spending time with the person? The body often knows before the mind does. Paying attention to these signals helps you notice which relationships bring ease and which bring strain.

Testing Safety Gradually

If supportive relationships feel unfamiliar, it's natural to test them slowly. You might share a small truth and see how the other person responds. If they listen and respond with care, you feel safer sharing more. Trust is built through these small moments, not grand declarations. Over time, these tests create a foundation of security, allowing you to open more fully.

Choosing Supportive Relationships

Part of healing is learning to choose connections that embody these qualities. This doesn't mean waiting for "perfect" people, but it does mean raising your standards. If someone consistently dismisses your feelings, violates your boundaries, or only takes without giving, you can choose to limit or end that relationship. At the same time, you can actively seek out connections with people who show care, consistency, and respect.

Safe and supportive relationships are not rare—they exist, but they may feel unfamiliar until you begin to recognize them. The more you practice noticing these qualities, the easier it becomes to trust them. And each supportive connection you nurture helps rewrite the old story that relationships are unsafe.

In these spaces, your inner child experiences something new: connection that doesn't demand self-betrayal. That experience alone is profoundly healing. It proves that love can coexist with respect, that belonging doesn't require performance, and that intimacy can feel safe.

The Role of Boundaries in Connection

At first, boundaries and connection may seem like opposites. Many people believe that boundaries push people away, creating walls that block intimacy. In reality, boundaries are what make intimacy possible. Without them, relationships slide into imbalance—one person gives too much, the other takes too much, and resentment grows in silence. Boundaries don't weaken connection; they protect it.

A boundary is simply a clear line that defines what is okay for you and what is not. It could be as straightforward as, *I need to leave by ten tonight,* or as emotional as, *I can't talk about that subject right now.* When you express these lines, you give others a chance to relate to the real you rather than a version of you who is suppressing needs to stay acceptable. That honesty is the foundation of authentic connection.

The absence of boundaries often feels like closeness at first. You say yes to everything, absorb others' moods, or sacrifice your time to keep the peace. On the surface, the relationship seems smooth, but underneath, resentment builds. Over time, that resentment leaks out in passive-aggressive comments, withdrawal, or exhaustion. Boundaries prevent this spiral by addressing issues early and directly. They allow small tensions to be resolved before they become heavy burdens.

Boundaries also model respect. When you say no with clarity and kindness, you teach others how to treat you. At the same time, when you respect others' boundaries, you show that you value their autonomy. This mutual respect strengthens trust. You both know that connection is a choice, not a demand.

In relationships where old wounds are triggered, boundaries are even more important. If you grew up with people who ignored your limits, asserting them now may feel frightening. The critic may warn, *If you set this boundary, they'll leave you.* And sometimes, people will resist. But the resistance is information: it shows you who can adapt to your authenticity and who cannot. Boundaries act as filters, revealing which relationships are capable of growth.

Practical communication helps boundaries work in daily life. Clear, short phrases reduce confusion: *I can't stay late tonight. I need some time alone. That doesn't work for me.* You don't need to defend your decision with endless explanations. The more simply you speak, the easier it is for others to understand. If someone pushes, you can repeat yourself calmly, like a steady reminder that your line is firm.

Boundaries do not erase flexibility. Sometimes you may choose to bend for someone you care about, knowing it won't harm you. The difference is that the choice comes from willingness, not fear. Flexibility without boundaries leads to burnout. Flexibility with boundaries leads to generosity that feels sustainable.

In the context of healing, boundaries are a way of reparenting yourself. Each time you set one, you tell your inner child: *I will protect you now. I won't let others cross lines that hurt you.* This consistency builds safety inside, even when the outside world remains unpredictable.

Relationships thrive when both people bring clear boundaries. Far from being a barrier, they create the conditions where honesty, respect, and trust can grow. When you know where you stand and others know where they stand, the space between you becomes a place of choice rather than compulsion. And choice is what makes connection real.

Letting Others In Without Losing Yourself

For many people who grew up people-pleasing, connection has always come at a cost. To belong, you had to silence parts of yourself. To be loved, you had to perform. Over time, closeness and self-betrayal became intertwined—you could have one, but not the other. Healing requires unlearning this equation. You can let others in without disappearing. You can be connected without losing yourself.

The fear of losing yourself often shows up when relationships deepen. You may start by feeling excited and open, but as the bond grows, anxiety creeps in: *What if I have to give too much? What if I can't keep them happy? What if being myself drives them away?* These fears are echoes of old experiences, not predictions of the future. The key is learning to stay rooted in your authenticity while allowing connection to unfold.

One way to do this is by checking in with yourself regularly. Before making commitments or responding to requests, pause and ask: *What do I truly want here? Does this choice align with my needs and values?* This practice ensures that your yes means yes and your no means no. It prevents the automatic compliance that once felt necessary for survival.

Boundaries, again, are central. Letting others in doesn't mean giving unlimited access. It means choosing how much of yourself to share, when, and with whom. This choice is not about building walls—it's about creating healthy doors. You decide who enters, how far, and under what conditions. When connection happens through choice instead of compulsion, it feels nourishing rather than draining.

It also helps to notice how your body feels in relationships. Do you feel relaxed, energized, and open around someone? Or do you feel tense, small, or constantly on guard? Your body often tells you whether a connection is safe. Trusting these signals allows you to discern which relationships deserve deeper access and which require distance.

Letting others in without losing yourself also means embracing vulnerability. Many people believe that protecting themselves means never showing weakness. But true protection comes from knowing you can reveal your feelings while still holding onto your boundaries. Saying, *I feel hurt,* or *I'm scared,* is not the same as surrendering yourself. It is sharing your truth while staying grounded in your own worth.

Relationships that support your authenticity will meet this vulnerability with care, not exploitation. If someone consistently dismisses or manipulates your openness, that's a signal to step back. Self-trust gives you the confidence to walk away from connections that demand your silence. Healing is not about forcing every relationship to work—it's about choosing the ones where you can stay whole.

Another practice is balancing giving and receiving. People-pleasers often default to giving, believing their value lies in what they provide. Letting others in means allowing yourself to receive, too: compliments, help, affection, support. Receiving without guilt teaches your inner child that you are worthy of care, not just for what you do but for who you are.

It's also important to accept that not every relationship will feel safe for full openness, and that's okay. Different connections serve different purposes. Some may be light and playful, others deeply intimate. What matters is that in each one, you stay connected to yourself. You can adapt without abandoning, adjust without erasing.

Over time, practicing these skills creates a new sense of balance. You no longer have to choose between isolation and self-betrayal. You learn to inhabit the middle ground—relationships where you can be both connected and authentic. In this space, intimacy becomes sustainable, because it does not require sacrifice.

Letting others in without losing yourself is one of the greatest gifts you can give your inner child. It proves that belonging no longer depends on erasure. It shows that closeness can coexist with integrity. And it opens the door to relationships that heal rather than wound—connections where you are loved not for the mask you wear, but for the person you truly are.

Chapter 10:
Creating a Life of Wholeness

Healing your inner child is not only about addressing wounds from the past. It is also about shaping the present and future into something that feels whole. Wholeness doesn't mean perfection. It doesn't mean you never feel pain, doubt, or conflict. Instead, it means living in alignment with yourself—your values, your emotions, your boundaries, and your joy. It is the steady sense that you are no longer divided against yourself.

For many people, life before healing feels fragmented. There is the public self that pleases others, the private self that hides in shame, and the wounded child within who longs for care. These parts often pull in different directions, leaving you exhausted and unsure who you really are. Wholeness is what happens when these parts begin to integrate. The inner child feels safe, the adult self feels grounded, and your outer life begins to reflect your inner truth.

Creating a life of wholeness requires intention. It does not happen by accident. It grows through daily choices that honor who you are becoming. One of those choices is authenticity—showing up as yourself, even when it feels risky. Each time you choose honesty over performance, you reinforce the belief that your truth is enough.

Another element of wholeness is balance. Healing the inner child often involves swinging between extremes: giving everything to others or withdrawing completely, suppressing emotions or being overwhelmed by them. Wholeness is not found in extremes but in integration. You learn to care for others without abandoning yourself, to feel deeply without being consumed, to rest without guilt and to work with purpose.

Relationships also play a role in wholeness. A whole life includes connections that nourish rather than drain, bonds where you can be both vulnerable and strong. This doesn't mean you will never face conflict or disappointment, but it does mean you choose relationships where your authenticity can survive. The quality of these relationships often shifts as you grow. Some old ties may loosen, while new ones emerge that reflect your truer self.

Self-trust remains central. Wholeness requires confidence that you can rely on yourself, even when circumstances are uncertain. This trust allows you to take risks, pursue dreams, and face challenges without crumbling. It is the anchor that steadies you when external validation falters.

Joy and play are also essential. Without them, life may feel stable but flat. Wholeness includes aliveness, moments of delight that remind you healing is not just about less pain but about more living. Whether through creativity, adventure, or simple pleasures, joy keeps the heart open.

Wholeness is also about purpose. This doesn't necessarily mean a grand mission or career path. It means orienting your life toward what matters most to you—whether that's raising a family, contributing to your community, creating art, or living simply and peacefully. Purpose gives direction, reminding you why healing is worth the effort.

Importantly, a life of wholeness is not free of struggle. Old wounds may resurface. The critic may still whisper. Setbacks may occur. But the difference is how you meet them. Instead of collapsing into shame or fear, you meet challenges with resilience. You know how to listen to your emotions, set boundaries, reach for support, and care for yourself. You know you will not abandon yourself again. That steady commitment is what makes you whole.

Creating wholeness is an ongoing process, not a final destination. You may never feel "done," but you will feel more integrated, more consistent, and more at peace. The fractured parts of you begin to work together rather than against each other. And in that integration, life feels fuller, richer, and more authentic.

In the end, a life of wholeness is not measured by external success or constant happiness. It is measured by alignment—the quiet knowledge that you are living in a way that honors both your inner child and your present self. It is the freedom to be imperfect and still worthy, to be vulnerable and still strong, to be authentic and still loved.

This is the promise of healing: not a life without pain, but a life where you can hold pain and joy together, without losing yourself to either. A life that feels steady, true, and whole.

Integrating the Inner Child and Adult Self

Healing often feels like a tug-of-war between different parts of yourself. On one side, the inner child longs for safety, joy, and validation. On the other, the adult self feels the weight of responsibility, decision-making, and survival. For many people, these two parts rarely communicate. The child feels silenced, while the adult feels burdened. Integration is the process of bringing them together, so that they no longer compete but cooperate.

Integration begins with recognition. The inner child is not a weakness or a flaw—it is the part of you that carries emotional memory, creativity, and vulnerability. The adult self is not a tyrant—it is the part of you that provides stability, protection, and structure. Both are essential. Healing requires listening to the child's needs while allowing the adult to guide choices.

A simple practice is to pause when strong emotions arise and ask: *What is my inner child feeling? What does my adult self know?* For example, if you feel anxious before a social event, the child may be afraid of rejection. The adult, however, knows that you have survived difficult moments before and can leave if the situation feels unsafe. When you allow both voices, you avoid either being swallowed by fear or dismissing your feelings entirely.

Integration also involves play. The inner child thrives on fun and creativity, while the adult often prioritizes efficiency. When you deliberately create space for joy—through hobbies, laughter, or adventure—you honor the child while reminding the adult that productivity is not the only measure of value. These moments bring balance, softening the adult's rigidity and affirming the child's right to joy.

Boundaries are another way integration shows up. The adult self sets and enforces limits, protecting the child from harm. Each time you say no to something that feels unsafe or overwhelming, you prove to the child: *I am here. I will keep you safe.* Over time, this consistency builds trust between these two parts, reducing inner conflict.

Integration is not about erasing differences but about building cooperation. The inner child reminds the adult to feel, to play, to imagine. The adult reminds the child that safety and structure exist. Together, they create wholeness—a self that is both tender and strong, playful and grounded.

Balancing Responsibility and Self-Care

One of the greatest challenges of adulthood is learning how to carry responsibility without losing yourself in the process. Bills must be paid, work must be done, children must be cared for, relationships require attention. These responsibilities are real, and ignoring them is not an option. But when responsibility consumes every ounce of energy, self-care is the first thing to disappear. The result is burnout, resentment, and the silent belief that your worth depends only on what you produce for others.

For those who grew up people-pleasing, this imbalance can feel especially familiar. As a child, you may have learned that your value came from taking care of others—keeping parents calm, smoothing over conflict, or excelling to earn approval. By the time you reach adulthood, responsibility feels natural, while self-care feels selfish. The critic reinforces this belief, saying, *You don't deserve rest until everything is finished.* But everything is never finished. Without conscious effort, self-care remains perpetually out of reach.

Balancing responsibility and self-care requires reframing both. Responsibility is not only about meeting obligations—it is also about sustaining yourself so that you can meet them well. Self-care is not indulgence—it is maintenance. Just as a car needs fuel and oil changes to keep running, you need rest, nourishment, and joy to function. Without them, responsibility eventually collapses under its own weight.

A practical first step is to schedule self-care as intentionally as you schedule work. This may feel uncomfortable at first, but treating self-care as optional ensures it never happens. Block time for rest, movement, or creative activities just as you would for meetings or errands. Protect that time with the same seriousness. Over time, this practice sends a powerful message: *My well-being is a responsibility too.*

Another strategy is learning to prioritize. Not every task carries equal importance, though the critic often insists it does. By identifying what truly matters—both in responsibilities and in self-care—you can distribute energy more wisely. Sometimes that means letting go of perfection, allowing "good enough" to replace constant striving. Other times it means saying no to requests that drain you, even if they once felt obligatory. Each no creates space for a more balanced yes.

Listening to your body is crucial in this balance. Fatigue, irritability, or restlessness are signals that self-care is overdue. Instead of overriding these cues with caffeine, distraction, or guilt, honor them. Pause and ask: *What do I need right now?* The answer may be as simple as water, a break, or a breath of fresh air. Responding to these needs strengthens self-trust and prevents the build-up of resentment.

Self-care doesn't always require large amounts of time. Small rituals woven into daily life can have enormous impact: a short walk after work, a quiet cup of tea, a few minutes of journaling before bed. These micro-moments remind you that your well-being matters even in the midst of busyness. They also counter the critic's narrative that self-care must be earned or scheduled only in long stretches.

Balancing responsibility and self-care also involves community. Sharing responsibilities with others—whether household tasks, emotional support, or childcare—creates more room for balance. Many people-pleasers hesitate to ask for help, fearing they'll be a burden. But allowing others to contribute strengthens relationships and models reciprocity. Self-care often becomes easier when responsibility is shared rather than carried alone.

It's important to recognize that balance is not a fixed state. Some seasons of life require more responsibility, others allow more self-care. The goal is not perfect equilibrium but ongoing adjustment. By checking in regularly—*Am I giving too much to responsibility right now? Am I neglecting care?*—you can make course corrections before burnout sets in.

Ultimately, balance is about honoring both sides of yourself: the adult who carries responsibility and the inner child who needs care. When you neglect one, the other suffers. But when you give both attention, life feels steadier. Responsibilities are met without resentment, and self-care becomes a natural part of daily rhythm.

This balance is a cornerstone of wholeness. It proves that you can be reliable without being depleted, caring without abandoning yourself, responsible without losing your spark. In honoring both responsibility and self-care, you create a life that is not only sustainable but deeply alive.

Living with Purpose and Alignment

Healing your inner child doesn't only mean addressing pain—it also means creating a life that feels meaningful. Without purpose, healing can feel incomplete, like patching holes without ever building a home. Purpose gives direction. Alignment gives steadiness. Together, they create the sense that your life reflects not just survival, but truth.

For many people, purpose is misunderstood. The critic insists it must be something dramatic: a career that changes the world, an accomplishment that wins admiration. But true purpose is often quieter. It is found in the values you live by, the relationships you nurture, the ways you contribute to others' lives in big or small ways. Purpose is not about proving your worth—it's about expressing it.

Living in alignment means your actions match your values. If you value honesty, you speak truth even when it's uncomfortable. If you value compassion, you choose kindness even in small interactions. If you value creativity, you make space for it regularly, even if no one else sees it. Alignment is not perfection—it's consistency. It's the daily decision to let your choices reflect who you truly are.

When you live out of alignment, life feels fractured. You say yes when you mean no. You pursue goals that impress others but leave you empty. You silence parts of yourself to maintain peace. The result is a lingering sense of disconnection, as if you are playing a role rather than living your life. The inner child feels this dissonance deeply, because it mirrors the old experience of being unseen.

Purpose and alignment don't need to arrive all at once. They grow through small questions: *What matters to me today? How can I live closer to that?* Some days, purpose may look like pursuing a dream. Other days, it may look like resting so you have the strength to keep going. Alignment is less about grand gestures and more about a steady accumulation of honest choices.

Journaling can help clarify values. Write about moments when you felt most alive, most at peace, or most proud. What qualities were present? What values were honored? These reflections often reveal patterns that point toward purpose. You may notice that creativity, service, connection, or freedom shows up again and again. Once identified, you can begin to build your daily life around them.

Living with purpose also means embracing imperfection. The critic may insist that unless you live your values perfectly, you're failing. But alignment is not about never straying—it's about noticing when you drift and returning gently. Each return strengthens self-trust and proves that purpose is not a rigid demand but a guiding light.

Relationships reflect alignment as well. When you live by your values, you naturally attract people who resonate with them and distance from those who do not. This can feel both liberating and painful. Some relationships may fade as you stop performing. But the ones that remain will feel deeper, built on truth rather than masks.

Ultimately, living with purpose and alignment is about integration. The inner child, once silenced, now has a voice in shaping your choices. The adult self, once overburdened, now feels guided rather than lost. Together, they create a life that feels whole.

Purpose is not about becoming someone else. It is about remembering who you are and letting that truth shape your days. Alignment is not about perfection. It is about choosing, moment by moment, to live honestly. And when you do, life begins to feel less like a performance and more like your own.

Sustaining Wholeness Over Time

Wholeness is not a one-time achievement. It's not a finish line you cross and never look back. It is a way of living—one that requires attention, practice, and patience. Old wounds don't vanish overnight, and the critic doesn't disappear completely. But with steady care, the balance you've built can last. Sustaining wholeness is about learning how to nurture it through daily choices and long-term perspective.

Expecting Ebbs and Flows

Healing does not follow a straight line. There will be times when you feel grounded, authentic, and at peace, and other times when old patterns resurface. The critic may get louder, or an unexpected trigger may stir up familiar pain. This doesn't mean you've failed. It means you are human. Expecting ebbs and flows helps you stay steady when difficulties return. Instead of panicking, you can remind yourself: *This is part of the process. I know how to care for myself now.*

Returning to Core Practices

Sustaining wholeness depends on small, consistent practices that keep you connected to yourself. Checking in with your emotions. Setting boundaries when needed. Making time for joy and rest. Journaling or reflecting on what feels aligned. These practices don't need to be perfect, but they need to be present. Each one is like tending a garden—small actions that, over time, create lasting growth.

Building Resilience Through Relationships

Safe relationships help sustain wholeness. When you are surrounded by people who respect your authenticity and honor your boundaries, you feel supported in living true to yourself. These relationships also provide reminders of your growth when you doubt it. A friend who says, *I can see how much stronger you've become,* or a partner who respects your no without question, reinforces the healing you've worked so hard for.

At the same time, sustaining wholeness means being discerning. Not every relationship can come with you into this new chapter. Some may continue to pull you toward old patterns of self-betrayal. Part of long-term healing is recognizing which connections nurture your wholeness and which erode it—and having the courage to act accordingly.

Keeping Joy Alive

Wholeness without joy quickly becomes survival mode. To sustain it, you need play, laughter, and creativity woven into your life. These moments of lightness don't erase responsibility—they balance it. Make joy part of your routine, not an afterthought. Whether it's music, art, nature, or humor, let delight be a regular visitor in your life. The more you practice joy, the more natural it becomes, even in hard seasons.

Guarding Against Perfectionism

The critic often tries to twist healing into another performance. It whispers, *You should have mastered this by now. You shouldn't feel pain anymore. You should be whole all the time.* This perfectionism is a trap. Sustaining wholeness means rejecting the idea that healing has to look flawless. You can stumble and still be whole. You can feel pain and still be healed. Wholeness is not about erasing struggle—it's about carrying it differently.

Honoring Change Over Time

Life will continue to evolve. New jobs, relationships, losses, and transitions will bring fresh challenges. Sustaining wholeness means adapting without losing yourself. The practices that work today may shift tomorrow. Staying flexible—open to change while rooted in your values—keeps you steady through life's unpredictability.

Trusting Yourself

At the core of sustaining wholeness is self-trust. You may not know what the future holds, but you know you will meet it with authenticity. You trust that you will listen to your emotions, care for your needs, and protect your inner child. This trust is what turns healing from a temporary breakthrough into a lifelong foundation.

In the end, sustaining wholeness is less about maintaining a perfect state and more about returning to yourself again and again. No matter what happens—triggers, setbacks, or challenges—you know the path back. And each return strengthens your resilience.

Wholeness is not a fragile achievement you must guard anxiously. It is a living practice, renewed daily through choice, care, and compassion. When you commit to sustaining it, you give your inner child the greatest gift: the assurance that they will never be abandoned again.

Conclusion

Healing your inner child is not a task you finish once and set aside. It is a lifelong relationship—a commitment to care for the parts of you that were silenced, ignored, or hurt. Over the course of these chapters, we've explored the critic, people-pleasing, boundaries, self-trust, joy, and relationships. Each piece is important, but together they point toward something larger: coming home to yourself.

For many years, home may not have felt safe. Your body may have carried tension, your mind may have been filled with self-doubt, and your heart may have felt guarded. To survive, you learned to leave yourself behind, chasing approval, avoiding rejection, or suppressing feelings. But survival is not the same as living. Healing invites you back inside, to reclaim the ground of your own being.

Coming home to yourself begins with listening. Listening to the child who once longed to be held, to the emotions that rise in your body, to the quiet voice that knows what feels true. This listening is radical because it interrupts years of conditioning. It says: *I matter. My needs are real. My feelings deserve respect.* Each act of listening builds a foundation of safety inside, one brick at a time.

It also involves protection. You protect your wholeness through boundaries, refusing to allow relationships or environments that demand your silence. Protection is not isolation—it is the choice to create conditions where you can thrive. Each time you say no to what harms you, you say yes to what heals you.

Joy, too, is part of this homecoming. Without it, healing risks becoming heavy, defined only by struggle. Joy reminds you that you are not only a survivor of pain but also a seeker of life. Whether through play, laughter, or creativity, joy reconnects you to the freedom you once knew as a child and still deserve today.

Relationships shape this journey as well. Healing does not happen in a vacuum. When you allow yourself to be seen in safe connections, you rewrite old stories of rejection and neglect. When you give and receive with balance, you prove that love can coexist with authenticity. The people who meet you in this truth become companions on your path, reflecting back the wholeness you are building.

Perhaps the most profound part of coming home is cultivating self-trust. Without it, healing feels fragile, dependent on external reassurance. With it, healing becomes resilient. Self-trust means knowing that no matter what happens, you will not abandon yourself again. You will listen, protect, and care for the child inside. That promise changes everything.

This book has offered tools and reflections, but healing will always unfold in your own way. There is no single path, no perfect timeline. Some days will feel like breakthroughs, others like setbacks. But both are part of the same movement toward integration. The fact that you are engaging in this work at all is evidence of courage—the courage to face what was once unbearable and to choose something different.

As you move forward, remember that wholeness is not a destination but a practice. You will revisit old wounds. You will catch yourself slipping into people-pleasing or harsh self-talk. You will feel the critic rise. These moments are not signs of failure. They are opportunities to return, to practice again, to strengthen the new patterns you are building. Each return makes the path smoother, each act of care more natural.

The gift of healing is not perfection. It is freedom—the freedom to live without constant fear of rejection, the freedom to rest without guilt, the freedom to love without losing yourself. It is the quiet confidence of knowing that you can face pain without being consumed by it and embrace joy without waiting for permission.

Your inner child has waited a long time for this. They have waited to be seen, heard, and loved by you. That love may feel awkward at first, but with time, it becomes second nature. And in that love, you find the wholeness that was missing—not because your wounds disappeared, but because you chose to live with them honestly, with care and with compassion.

So as you close these pages, the work does not end. It continues in your choices today, tomorrow, and every day after. In the way you speak to yourself, in the boundaries you set, in the joy you allow, in the trust you build. Each choice is another step home.

Coming home to yourself is the greatest act of healing. It is the promise that you will no longer abandon the child inside, that you will honor both your vulnerability and your strength. It is living not as a fractured self but as a whole one—imperfect, authentic, and free.

And that, more than anything, is the life you deserve.

About the Author

Nancy Willis is a writer, speaker, and mentor dedicated to helping others heal the invisible wounds of childhood and reclaim their authentic selves. After years of her own struggle with people-pleasing, self-doubt, and the quiet pain of never feeling "enough," Nancy discovered the power of inner child work and the profound transformation that comes from learning to listen inward.

Drawing from both personal experience and years of study in psychology, self-development, and trauma recovery, she brings a compassionate, down-to-earth voice to the journey of healing. Her work is guided by the belief that true growth does not come from striving for perfection but from learning to trust ourselves, set boundaries with confidence, and allow joy back into our lives.

Nancy's writing blends gentle insight with practical tools, helping readers move beyond survival into a life of wholeness. She is passionate about creating spaces—on the page and in her workshops—where people feel seen, validated, and empowered to change the patterns that once kept them stuck.

When she isn't writing or teaching, Nancy enjoys long walks in nature, painting, and sharing laughter with her close circle of family and friends. She lives with gratitude for the ordinary moments that remind her daily of the joy and freedom that come with healing.

Her deepest hope is that readers of her work not only find comfort but also feel the courage to embrace themselves fully—past, present, and future.

www.ingramcontent.com/pod-product-compliance
Lightning Source LLC
Chambersburg PA
CBHW050220270326
41914CB00003BA/504